"Dr. Swenson is an unusually gifted writer, teacher, and interpreter of our times. Drawing upon Scripture, history, and his own experiences, he has fashioned a book that confronts the dehumanizing dimensions of twenty-first-century culture that drive so many people to anxiety, depression, and despair. A first-rate physician, Dr. Swenson offers us prescriptions from the Bible that will help us see how God at once calls us to contentment and shows us how to get there. This is a book we need to listen to and share with others."
—REVEREND DR. LYLE DORSETT, Billy Graham professor of evangelism, Beeson Divinity School of Samford University

"Lost your joy? Have no peace? With wisdom, wit, and discernment, Dr. Swenson leads us down the hidden path to serenity, happiness, and satisfaction. In these chaotic times, we need to practice the principles he prescribes daily. It's exactly the medicine we need to experience contentment. Don't miss this journey!"
—DAVID L. STEVENS, MD, CEO, Christian Medical and Dental Society

"Ever the family physician, Dr. Swenson guides us in embracing a lifelong lifestyle change guaranteed to improve our quality of life and relationships with both people and God. This book is counterintuitive to the pace and direction of life today but is the kind of life-giving information you want to hear and share. *Contentment* is more than a book to be read; it is to be heeded and applied."
—DR. GARY BENEDICT, president, Christian and Missionary Alliance, U.S.

"If contentment comes from deciding not to yearn for what I cannot have, deciding to take steps to free myself of some of the things I do have, and deciding to enjoy what remains, then Dr. Richard Swenson provides a rich garden of reasons to make those decisions, an arsenal of practical ways to implement them, and a compelling motivation to live a life within them. For the sake of the kingdom and the vitality of the church, I hope this book becomes a classic in the tradition of Christian spirituality."
—WALTER J. SCHULTZ, PhD, professor of philosophy, Northwestern College

CONTENTMENT

The Secret to a Lasting Calm

RICHARD A. SWENSON, MD

NAVPRESS®

A NavPress resource published in alliance
with Tyndale House Publishers, Inc.

NAVPRESS◐®

NavPress is the publishing ministry of The Navigators, an international Christian organization and leader in personal spiritual development. NavPress is committed to helping people grow spiritually and enjoy lives of meaning and hope through personal and group resources that are biblically rooted, culturally relevant, and highly practical.

For more information, visit www.NavPress.com.

Library of Congress Cataloging-in-Publication Data

Swenson, Richard A.
  Contentment : the secret to a lasting calm / Richard A. Swenson, MD.
    pages cm
  Includes bibliographical references and index.
  ISBN 978-1-61747-182-7
  1. Contentment—Religious aspects—Christianity. I. Title.
  BV4647.C7S94 2013
  241'.4—dc23

                              2013002545

Printed in the United States of America

21 20 19 18 17
10 9 8 7 6 5

OTHER BOOKS BY DR. RICHARD A. SWENSON

In Search of Balance

Margin

A Minute of Margin

More Than Meets the Eye

The Overload Syndrome

Restoring Margin to Overloaded Lives

To Linda

Loving, patient co-laborer in the writing life for thirty years . . .
a life impossible to imagine under any other terms

CONTENTS

ACKNOWLEDGMENTS

Writing, at least in my case, is a profoundly solitary experience: agonizing, up-till-dawn, drawn out, all else cast aside. That said, writing is also a privilege and a calling. At the end of every night, the question must be asked: Where did these words come from? At the end of every book, the question must be answered: Creativity is a gift from above. Yet, even in my isolation, God has ordained that such creativity be supported by others beyond my own efforts.

First in line, as always, is Linda. Although it is impossible to fully explain the material in my spirit struggling for expression, she understands it better than all others combined. She does not chide my groaning nor when we have breakfast at midnight nor when my research area looks like a bomb went off, and she is my biggest affirmer, corrector, editor, researcher, and encourager. Impossibly, Linda goes over the manuscript again and again, tirelessly, each time finding something to be set right. Other family members follow closely, Matt and Suzie, Adam, Maureen, Katja, Caroline, Karen, Marcia and Jerry, Hazel, Paul and Comfort, Tom and Vicki, Heather and Ron, each contributing in their various ways.

Jack and Diana, even the extreme distance did not stop nor slow your interest and prayers. Allison and Brent, you both contributed in ways that made a difference. Bill and Gail, know you are always appreciated. Beth Rubusch, your specific and timely prayers aid us in extraordinary ways. Sincere thanks also flow to Kris, Donna, Aggie, Roger and Joanne, Hector, Kathryn, Opal, Debbie, Marilynn, and Loretta Hoover. Don Simpson, you are a patient and wise saint. Arvid Wallen, thank you for the inspired cover design, my favorite over a two-decade span. Kris, Tia, Erica, and all at NavPress, thank you once again.

CHAPTER 1

THE FREEDOM OF CONTENTMENT

A Gift from Another World

We are spiritual beings having a physical experience.

— DALLAS WILLARD

Katja, our seven-year-old granddaughter, stepped in it, as they say. She had doggie droppings on the bottom of her tennies. Not just one foot, mind you, but both. Her mother, Maureen, suggested she leave the shoes outside, where they could be cleaned after lunch.

An hour later, Adam and Katja went for a walk to fix the problem. She put on her shoes, looked for a good stick, and off they went down the street. When they came to an appropriate spot, she sat on the curb and started scraping. Thirty seconds later, she stopped. She looked up at Adam with a smile, down at her shoes, then at the brown stuff scraped onto the street.

"You know, Daddy," she said, "this would make a very good meal for a dung beetle."

The contentment range of unspoiled children is a mile from end to end. Joy beacons, I call them, God's little ambassadors to cheerless cynics. The laughter of just one child is enough to lift a crowd of fifty.

Where do they get this capacity? How do they pull it off so casually, to make happy connections between a shoe full and the disgusting culinary habits of ugly beetles? According to statistics, four-year-olds laugh 26.6 times more than I do. No wonder Jesus preferred the kids to, say, me. To be honest, I prefer them to me too.

Young children find equal delight in a puddle or a pigeon, a worm or a waffle. Throw in a puppy, and joy goes off the charts. "The kingdom of heaven belongs to such as these."[1]

Contentment in the young does not require Disneyland. Just a book on beetles. Or a puppet drinking green milk. Just hearts with the capacity for delight, brains with the capacity for imagination, and spirits with the innocence of sufficiency.

Perhaps the statute of limitations for creation wonder has not yet expired for them. Maybe in some mystical way they retain the slightest inkling of what it was like when light and energy and glory and love burst upon a microscopic spot, and suddenly they were, when before they were not.

But now they live below, where the world is too much with us. Whatever the source of their naissant contentment and joy, it begins to fade. Before long, they join the rest of us for whom contentment is a difficult reach.

THE JOY OF CONTENTMENT

Contentment is one of the greatest joys and privileges of the Christian life. "The Lord is my shepherd, *I shall not want*" is God speaking code about a secret path (yes, it is a secret) to freedom. Freedom from wanting more than is good for us. Freedom to wish blessing on everyone we meet without the slightest tinge of envy. Freedom to redefine wealth and possessions in biblical rather than cultural terms. Freedom to gladly surrender our strife and have it replaced by His rest. Freedom to be biblically authentic in an age of financially-forced compromises. Freedom to understand that one heart, inhabited by Christ, is enough to take on the world's opinion machine.

God takes care to describe Himself as a shepherd in both testaments. The ancient world understood that when the shepherd loves his flock, the sheep are contented. They rest in peace, unafraid. It is the shepherd who names them and talks to them, who provides for their needs, who fights their predators, who sacrifices for them. It is the shepherd in Psalm 23 who brings the flock to an oasis, a place of still waters and green pastures where they "lack nothing," where he restores their soul, or, more literally, "causes their life to return."

Sometimes contentment comes when we are tired of being wounded by the world, exhausted trying to measure up and keep up and buck up. We limp to the Shepherd with tears in our eyes. We see Him then, not as somebody who wants to force us to do something we don't want to do, but as somebody who has something we desperately need.

Contentment is when we tell the Shepherd that *His provision is enough for all our physical and material needs*. If our old car gimps down the road, that is fine. If we get a shiny newer auto with less gimp, that too is fine. Because it is not about the cars. My contentment is unaltered in any circumstance, because the Shepherd is the source of my provision and He doeth all things well.

Contentment is when we tell the Shepherd that *His presence is sufficient for all our emotional needs*. We seek solutions for our emptiness in many directions, all of them lacking. But those who go deep with Jesus discover He is always better. The greater our intimacy, the greater our contentment.

Contentment is when we tell the Shepherd that *His providence is perfect for all our future needs*. Despite the uncertainty and turmoil of our age, God knows what He is doing, holds time in His hand, has never failed, and is our friend. Contentment opens the door with welcome to receive whatever blessing or hardship God sends, knowing He sends both as needed with precision.

If I haven't been sick a day in my life, that is fine. If my biopsy comes back indicating the worst, that too is fine, because God inspired the "in sickness and in health" clause, and He knows how to carry us through good times and bad.

If my lot in life is low, I rejoice because "it is enough to exist for the glory of God alone."[2] If my station in life is high, I rejoice knowing it is not for my station that I love Him, but simply because He is my Shepherd and I am part of His flock. "God's end in all His cross providences is to bring the heart to submit and be content," wrote Thomas Watson (1620–1686). "And, indeed, this pleases God much. He loves to see His children satisfied with that portion He carves and allots them. It contents Him to see us content."

Despite having fallen out of favor in modern times, contentment is such a prominent theme of Scripture that we are constrained by the sacred words to reconsider our neglect. Ignoring God's instruction leads to the kind of desperate troubles in which we now find ourselves.

TWO REALITIES

We live in two worlds. This is constant and continuous. We have no choice. If we take a step in either world, we take a step in both worlds.

One world is small, the other much larger. One is limited, the other unlimited.

The first world, the smaller one, is the one we know so well. It is right in front of us and all around us. We can see it, hear it, smell it, and touch it. This world, this reality, is straightforward and quickly discerned by our senses.

The second world, the larger one, is far more interesting but less discernable. We perceive it only vaguely, and at times, not at all. This is God's reality, the narrative where He lives. And it is veiled from us, for good reason.

The two worlds are in constant contact. Nothing that happens in our sub-reality escapes notice in God's dominant reality. Every action we take has meaning in both worlds. Every step here is a step there. Every word uttered here echoes throughout heaven.

The communication goes in both directions. Heaven might be hidden, but it is not silent. We should never mistake the subtleness of God's voice for the absence of His attention—nor the hiding of His action for the absence of His power. God speaks into my life just when I need it. I might have strife here, but I am offered contentment from there.

THE TUNNEL

We might think of our world as a tunnel. We journey through the tunnel but only in one direction, the same direction as time. God's reality sits above our reality, but it includes our tunnel. When my journey is ended, I will disappear through the wall and step into God's reality. When that happens, I will actually be *more* alive than I am now, not less. When we take into account both realities, there is no such thing as death.

As we live each day in our earthly corridor, sometimes we see glimmers of brightness along the walls. These glimmers remind us that our tunnel walls are not made of lead or steel but more like some type of clouded glass. We try to look out but can only "see through a glass, darkly."[3] Even so, these glimmers inflame our spiritual senses. The times we feel most alive in this world are the times we feel most connected to the other world.

This double narrative exists throughout the Scriptures. Jesus, more than anyone, understood the two realities. While teaching near the temple, He said, "You are from below; I am from above. You are of this world; I am not of this world."[4] He came to rescue us and to carry us safely from our tunnel into His realm. He also came to teach us about heaven and how to trust the Father and follow His will rather than the will of our corrupted world. He tried to teach us how to think in heavenly terms. Knowing what it was like on the other side, He could say outrageous things with complete calmness and credibility. *Love your enemies. Don't worry about tomorrow. Blessed are the persecuted.* Who talks like this except someone from another world?

The contentment theme in this book can be viewed from these two very different perspectives: (1) our view of things and (2) God's view of things. Understanding these two realities is important—perhaps essential—to getting contentment right. We can't hope to understand a heavenly concept without having a heavenly perspective.

From God's side, He knows exactly what He is doing. From our side, often we don't know what He is doing or why He is doing it. God can see into our world, but we can't see into His world. Until the redemption of all things is complete, the veil must remain.

This, of course, is the purpose of faith—a temporary bridge over this divide. When we are with God in heaven, we will no longer need faith for we will see Him face-to-face. However, in the tunnel, faith is essential.[5] I'm not referring to a faith empty of content but rather a faith rich in "evidence of things not seen."[6] God has supplied abundant evidences through the Scriptures, the Spirit, the lives of saints, our worship experiences, our private walk with Christ, and the natural revelation of God surrounding us—all making God's invisible attributes to be clearly apparent.[7] The witness is loud as a bullhorn. How can we ask God to be more explicit?

If we ask for the fullness of God's glory to manifest itself, it would be like telling people to stare at the sun. Our sun is lovely, but if we all stared at it, the human race would go blind. In the same way, people cannot see the full glory of God. It is not time. It would destroy the plan of salvation by taking away human choice. In addition, we are not equipped to see God face-to-face in our unglorified state, any more than we are equipped to stare into the sun. "You cannot see my face," God said to Moses, "for no one may see me and live."[8]

During this interim of hiddenness, it is our privilege to trust Him in all things. Contentment is but an extension of that trust. Kicking and screaming lead to misery, and it is foolish to be miserable when we could be trusting and content. God is never cruel, so what benefit is there in accusing Him of being insensitive or malicious? Has He not proven Himself on Golgotha?

SCIENCE AND SUGAR

Modern science understands the two realities well. The material world is more illusory and reality is more mystical than we think they are.

Science has very fuzzy peripheries. Discussing science over dinner with an MIT physics professor turned physician, after three hours I asked, "Is there any one thing in physics you know absolutely for sure?" He thought for a moment and then said, "No."

The material world is constructed from strange ingredients. Nothing is as it seems. Did you know, for example, that all of humanity can fit into a sugar cube? Just remove the space from everyone's body. It turns out that humans are 99.9999999999999 percent space. It is only the forces of physics that hold us together. The amount of matter in a human body is invisible, even to a microscope.

The Scriptures say that God spoke and the universe showed up, which is one hundred million trillion trillion trillion trillion grams. How many grams have humans created? Zero. Not a single one. The laws of science will not allow it.

The human brain weighs three pounds. Many scientists, well impressed by their fifty-ounce brains, have made it their goal to sit in judgment on God. In reality, they don't even know how their toasters work.

Perhaps you sense what I am driving at. I am a scientist and love science. Science is fun and can help our lives tremendously. But we shouldn't base our lives on science. It is merely "an orderly arrangement of what seem at the time to be facts." God is far more real and evident than that. All the important action happens not because of science on this side of the veil but because of spiritual realities on the other side, in God's domain. We do well to comprehend this as best we can because it plays a major role in our contentment. Judgments on our side are flawed; judgments on God's side are perfect.

In our world, we see but shadows on the wall; in God's world, we see face-to-face. In our world, we believe that a lifetime is eighty years; in God's world, we learn that life is a vapor. In our world, suffering is interminable; in God's world, suffering is momentary. In our world, everything is veiled; in God's world, everything is revealed. In our world, everything is tainted; in God's world, everything is pure.

We think we understand what is happening when in fact we do not. We only know a few details within our immediate awareness and, just as with science, even these are more indeterminate than we suspect.

Only God understands the full story. Only God is capable of acting with sufficient power to bring all things to conclusion. It is best that we trust Him with not only managing eternity but also the details of our lives. I rest content under the care of the Shepherd. No one else can get it right.

TIME AND TRANSCENDENCE

Time, too, does not exist in the way we think of it. It also has two realities. On the one hand, we think of time as fixed. The twenty-four-hour day is precisely twenty-four hours, down to the exact second. That is what our clocks say.

On the other hand, time is also elastic. It varies with regard to velocity and gravity, for example. If we increase our speed, time will begin to slow. When we accelerate to the speed of light, time will stand still. It will disappear.

Time has a strange way of merging with itself, causing Einstein to say, "People like us, who believe in physics, know that the distinction between the past, the present, and the future is only an illusion, even if a stubborn one." So, last year, next year, and now are . . . the same?

Decade after decade, Paul was beat up, bruised, and bloodied. Why did he then write that our troubles are momentary?[9] Because our troubles *are* momentary. This is not a trick of science or semantics — it's the truth. And it's a pretty good deal when you think about it.

We are trapped in time. We cannot stop it. We cannot back it up and will never be able to. God, however, created time. He is trapped by nothing, including time. He plays with it continuously. God is equally close to all points of history and geography — He is as close to Handel, as He is to you, as He is to your unborn great-grandchild.

Science is much stranger than most know, but isn't it exhilarating? The field of scientific knowledge which we have come to regard as cold and rigid is, in fact, wonderfully pliant in conforming to the miraculous nature of God's eternity.

Given our limited awareness, are we really capable of determining contentment on our own? For example, do we know enough to label something a failure? We should never call anything a failure until God has spoken. We dare not label our work, our lives, our kids, our churches, or our world as failures until God pounds the gavel. Massive surprises await us, perhaps in this life, surely in the next.

OUR PART IN ALL THINGS

The essence of reality is nonmaterial. Even in our tunnel, which is a material world, even here the essence of most activity is nonmaterial. Let's be perfectly clear: The secret world is real. It is with us, it is pervasive, and it is powerful. God is spirit, hidden but active. So is the Evil One.

Just because there is a hidden parallel world with great power working on our behalf, however, is no excuse for us to sit around doing nothing. That is not contentment. Even if most of the activity happening in any given moment is in the unseen world, we still have our part in all things.

God has given us abilities, strength, and intelligence. He has given us access to spiritual power through love, prayer, and the Word. In return, He expects us to seek out His agenda and cooperate with the Spirit's activities. All this implies effort on our part.

In all that lies ahead, contentment plays a role. We trust God completely, knowing He is continuously active in the shaping of not only history but our lives as well and realizing it is impossible for Him to make a mistake.

Some people, however, have a misunderstanding about how this concept works. They think because God is powerful and perfect, we are just along for the ride with limited responsibilities and decisions. On the contrary, contentment has nothing to do with inactivity or resignation. God expects us to work hard and seek to be successful at what He has set before us. Our good efforts please Him.

Contentment is not complacency in the face of things that should be changed. If we have a spiteful job where the boss is abusive, the hours are impossible, and the wages are meager, then, by all means, look for other work. God is our Father and He wishes us to thrive in our activities, not spend three decades chained in misery to a detestable job.

Contentment is not about mediocrity either. If we want to plant a flower garden, it is not sufficient to throw seeds on the ground and retire to the television for a month. We must work to make the flowers remind the world that God is a relentless artist.

Having said this, our own efforts today often exceed the requirements of contentment. We push and strive not for righteousness or the glory of God, but for inordinate personal desires that have nothing to do with the kingdom. We work perhaps for vanity, envy, or the love of money, and we often bypass God in our efforts to secure our own futures.

Contentment means we work hard on this broken world but always with a yielding to God in our hearts, a glad submission to His will, and a quiet confidence that as we do our part, God will do His part. Contentment is pursuing God's daily agenda even if it means walking directly into the storm. We know He is smarter than we are, and He cares for us more than we care for ourselves.

STARTING TO OPEN UP

A few years ago, a pastor friend died from stomach cancer. In his last week, he drifted into a stupor and then a coma. The day before he died, however, he sat up in bed, lifted his hands, and said, "It is starting to open up."

As he slipped through the wall of the tunnel, I doubt he argued with God about his cancer. He was not in the habit of murmuring against his Maker.

Life here is not the final reality. When God gets up from the sitting room of heaven and turns off His TV, everything we know will disappear and the dominant reality will take over. The *glass darkly* will become *face-to-face*.[10] This is what our friend was beginning to witness.

During the interim, we have a choice. We can live with discontentment, relentlessly striving after dissatisfactions we can scarcely name. Or we can choose to live with contentment and calmness, to accept adversity with peace, to "rest in the shadow of the Almighty,"[11] to have faith in God's plan for our lives, to believe God knows precisely what He is doing, to trust that He has considered every possibility and chosen the right course for us.

Corrie ten Boom is famous for her wise words, kindly demeanor, and amazing testimony of faith during WWII. When German troops occupied the Netherlands, the entire Ten Boom family began hiding Jews and other refugees in their home. Discovered by the Nazis in 1944, they were sent to a concentration camp.

Corrie's eldest sister, Betsie, sickly her entire life with pernicious anemia and now in her fifties, possessed an almost impossibly deep faith. When their barracks became infested with fleas, Betsie thanked God for the pests. Corrie, however, felt such piety stretched too far. She trusted God above all, but thanksgiving for fleas was a bit much.

The guards, it turned out, agreed with Corrie — about the fleas, that is. They hated them too. As a result, they stopped checking their barracks. And so it was that Betsie and Corrie could keep their Bibles, be together as sisters, pray, teach, and encourage others.

Contentment in a concentration camp with an infestation of fleas. How could victory be wrapped in a more unlikely package? Only the unseen world could have arranged such a thing.

CHAPTER 2

JESUS AND CONTENTMENT

The Man Who Needed Nothing

> When God made his strange invasion of this planet, he taught that what is apparently happening may bear little or no reality to what is really happening.
>
> — J. B. PHILLIPS

Jesus was not a normal person. Obviously, I do not mean He was abnormal. He was not weird or strange. It is just that He was not your usual human. He looked the part, of course, and He lived up to the "fully man" description. If He was a scholar, He was also a carpenter with the calluses to prove it. We know He liked to hang with fishermen, a trait that endears Him to my friends in Wisconsin. He was comfortable in the elements, with distant walks, with toughing it out when it got hot or cold, when the road was long and rainy and it was late at night and everyone was hungry. He could get up early in the morning while it was still dark to pray by Himself. He could sleep on the boat through the winds and the waves, no problem. He could do all that. He was not a wimp, did not grouse or complain.

But when I say He was not a normal person, I am speaking of

something more than a rustic hardiness. For example, He was unusual in that He never asked for advice. Jesus gave advice, but He did not take advice. This does not imply He was arrogant, for He was meek and a servant to all. But Jesus did not *need* advice. He did not *need* counsel from His disciples.

We are now getting closer to my meaning that Jesus was not a normal person. He was not normal because *He did not need things.* And that is an interesting character trait to explore in a book on contentment.

Jesus walked free of encumbrance. He had a holy disregard for the external. He spent an entire lifetime content with what He had and spoke against those who desired excess or cherished material things above spiritual things. His needs? By our standards, scandalously few.

For example, Jesus did not seem to *need* information, and He did not *need* to ask questions. We ask questions because we don't know something or because we're confused or perhaps afraid. Discontented people, in particular, ask lots of questions. But Jesus was not like that. He never asked, "Should we go to Jerusalem next week, or do you think it is too dangerous?" He never turned to John and said, "Who is that man over there?" He never conducted a survey to tell Him what His core values were. He only asked questions when He found them useful in teaching about the Law and the Prophets, about who He was, and about who we are.

When the great crowds approached Jesus, He turned to Philip and said, "'Where shall we buy bread for these people to eat?' He asked this only to test him, for he already had in mind what he was going to do."[1] After the Resurrection, Jesus asked Peter three times, "Peter, do you love me?"[2] However, He already knew the answer—He just wanted Peter to say it. When traveling by Caesarea Philippi, He asked the disciples, "Who do people say the Son of Man is?" But He asked the question only to pose the next: "Who do you say I am?"[3] He asked the two men on the road to Emmaus, "What are you discussing together as you walk along?"[4] even though He knew precisely what they were discussing. He simply wanted to open their eyes so they might later say, "Were not our hearts burning within us while he talked with us on the road and opened the Scriptures to us?"[5]

Jesus did not *need* shelter. It is hard to be precise about this because we know so little about where He slept. Was it a house? If so, most think it was Peter's house, although it is possible Jesus had a house of His own.[6] But if that were the case, shouldn't His house show up in the narrative at some point? Perhaps He slept out of doors or in a tent. Doesn't it seem strange that we learn virtually nothing regarding such a fundamental question? In our world, we want to see the houses of famous people. We try to drive past them; maybe have a walk through. If we tour Ephesus, they will show where the apostle John lived with Mary, Jesus' mother. Visit Capernaum and they will point out where Peter's house was. But the house of Jesus? That's not on any tour. The closest we come to specific information about where Jesus slept is when He said, "Foxes have dens and birds have nests, but the Son of Man has no place to lay his head."[7]

Jesus did not *need* money. We hardly ever see Him interacting with money except to issue a warning against its power. Did Jesus pay for His food? If so, where did He get the money? Did the disciples provide it? Did He live on donations? Were money and food simply given to Him by admirers? We know some followers were helping support Him out of their own means.[8] Another time, a fish donated money for the temple tax.[9] Still, these sources of provision hardy seem sufficient to account for three and a half years of ministry. Isn't it strange that we learn almost nothing about such things except that Judas Iscariot was the keeper of the purse?[10]

In our world, we need money for everything. We talk money, we think money, we sleep money, we dream money. Most of us don't know how to do much of anything except make money. We can't raise sheep, shear them, spin yarn, or weave cloth. We can't cut trees into boards, and we can't nail boards into houses. We don't know how to dig a well or plumb a house. I have a physics degree, but I can't build a car. Nor an egg timer for that matter. We are stuck—we need money or we perish. But Jesus did not *need* money.

Jesus did not *need* to have respectable parents. He chose, instead, a truly scandalous couple—a young unwed mother and a confused, disgraced father a long way from home with a lot of explaining to do when he got back. They were both righteous, of course, and chosen by God specifically for this task, which just goes to show that God did not *need* the well-bred, the aristocratic, or the elite for the most important parenting job in history.

Jesus did not *need* a luxurious birthing suite with Jacuzzi in a modern hospital. Doesn't it almost seem He required virtually nothing for His birth? He was just born. Mary pushed, Jesus came, and that was it. I am not suggesting that the stable and manger were random. They were not. The location was a divine choice as a statement that Jesus did not *need* any birthing preparation beyond what the Father had already provided for all babies.

Jesus did not *need* to be raised in a respectable town. "Nazareth!" Nathanael said. "Can anything good come from there?"[11] Nazareth's reputation was the worst in Galilee. Talk about the wrong side of the tracks. The Nazarenes even scorned the Messiah raised in their midst, did not believe Him, and tried to throw Him off a cliff.[12] No matter. Jesus did not *need* to hail from the best of places. Nathanael later changed his mind in mere seconds, for when he saw Jesus, he declared, "Rabbi, you are the Son of God; you are the king of Israel."[13]

Jesus did not *need* prestigious schools. Paul had a scholarly curriculum vitae, a record of achievement from the best institutions of learning. He was trained in the most prominent of rabbinical schools, was well versed in the Greek, Roman, and Hebrew worlds, and was both a Pharisee and a Roman citizen. Jesus was different. He studied presumably in His own nondescript synagogue. He had no educational degree. He left no written documents. He traveled little. Yet "the Jews there were amazed and asked, 'How did this man get such learning without having been taught?'"[14]

Jesus did not *need* good connections. He shunned high society, challenged the rich, and endlessly annoyed the religious hierarchy. No way around it—Jesus was tough on the privileged classes. The crowds

He preferred were all lower status: the poor, weak, handicapped, and sick. He loved children, of course. He appreciated laborers, such as carpenters, fishermen, farmers, and shepherds. He was seen eating with tax collectors and was not afraid of "women of reputation" and other sinners. As a result, onlookers were constantly critical of His acquaintances. It made no difference, for He did not *need* the good opinion of others.

Jesus, however, *did* need food and water. He was fully human and, as such, required what fully human people require, food and water chief among them. Nevertheless, He refocused even this need. When the disciples came out of a town and approached Him, they said,

> "Rabbi, eat something."
>
> But he said to them, "I have food to eat that you know nothing about."
>
> Then his disciples said to each other, "Could someone have brought him food?"
>
> "My food," said Jesus, "is to do the will of him who sent me and to finish his work."[15]

Another time, in the wilderness, He refocused the issue of food even more starkly.

> After fasting forty days and forty nights, he was hungry. The tempter came to him and said, "If you are the Son of God, tell these stones to become bread."
>
> Jesus answered, "It is written: 'Man shall not live on bread alone, but on every word that comes from the mouth of God.'"[16]

So Jesus did need food, but He controlled His need and would take food only under acceptable conditions.

Jesus *needed* clothes and sandals as well. But these items were simple and commonplace, culturally understood, not important in context, and thus never described. Only at His crucifixion do we finally see His robe and garments. Come to think of it, I am not sure I can name even one thing Jesus owned other than His clothes and sandals.

Jesus did not *need* to be handsome and well-groomed. Isn't it stunning that we know nothing about what Jesus looked like? How is this possible? It's not as if the Bible refuses to describe its characters. Saul was handsome and a head taller than everyone else. David was handsome and ruddy with a fine appearance. Absalom was more handsome than anyone in Israel, with no blemish from head to foot, and hair that was to die for. Zacchaeus was short and had to climb a tree to see Jesus.[17]

But the Messiah, the Savior of the world, God among us? We know nothing of His appearance except a brief veiled (and unflattering) description in Isaiah 53.[18] Are you ever curious? Was He handsome or plain? What color were His eyes? We assume He had a beard, but was it trimmed or long? Was His hair curly or straight, long or short? How tall was He? Was He muscular? Given that He is the central character in all of history, it is strange we know so little about these things.

Is it possible that if God had allowed Himself to be physically described, we would first have obsessed about it and then corrupted it? A danger lurks at the edges of this question, that many of us would soon have been more focused on His looks than on His message.

The record of Jesus described above could not be more different from our attitudes today. We have an insatiable interest for details about famous people. Television and magazines are filled with the minutiae of their lives. Yet these same particulars held zero interest for the writers of the Gospels. We don't know Jesus' address, His appearance, His clothes, His shoes, His hair, His education, or His income. The few things we know about are specifically intended to be unimpressive: His parents, His birthplace, His hometown, His connections.

This is beginning to sound a bit frightening in its implications. The things we clamor to know today about celebrities—and to be honest, about everybody—are precisely the details God hides from us concerning Jesus. Perhaps God is sending a message that our focus is wrong.

Perhaps He is saying we should be less interested in a person's looks, height, hair, and clothing, and more interested in his heart, spirit, and faith. Perhaps He wants us to close our eyes to a person's external appearance and open our hearts to that person's internal character. Perhaps credentials, privilege, possessions, and income don't actually mean that much to God.

If we began to emphasize the same attributes the Bible emphasizes with Jesus, it would constitute a massive shift in our collective thinking. If Jesus so clearly disregards external variables, we should also have a measured nonchalance regarding external particulars in our own lives: looks (height, weight, hair, attractiveness), clothes, houses, cars, jewelry, possessions, income.

If we were to put everything in our outer life on one list, and then do the same for our inner life, which list would Jesus focus on? The truth is so unambiguous that even kindergartners know the answer. Why, then, do we stubbornly refuse to change our thinking? Why do we wrongly insist on staring at the outside in direct defiance of Jesus Himself? If we all agreed to abide by the Savior's words and example and, in so doing, regard the things about a person that matter most to God, just imagine *how much easier and widespread biblical contentment would be.*

Needing things and possessing things were not a high priority for Jesus. This fact, however, is not to be a historical footnote forgotten among the temptations of modern life. *Everything Jesus did* has a continuing purpose in our own lives today, and *the way Jesus did everything* is a message that echoes across the ages to those of us who follow Him. The Messiah continues to send us signals. Wise people know when to pay attention.

In Deuteronomy, Moses gave final instructions to the children of Israel regarding a king. Be sure to let God choose the king, he said. Furthermore, the king "must not acquire great numbers of horses for himself. . . . He must not take many wives, or his heart will be led astray. He must not accumulate large amounts of silver and gold."[19] In summary, the king needed to be the kind of person who would limit military might (horses), physical pleasure or foreign alliances (wives), and wealth (gold or silver).

How about Jesus, who was not only a king but also a prophet and a priest? He had no horses, no wives, no gold, and no silver — because He did not *need* horses, military might, wives, physical pleasure, foreign alliances, gold, silver, or wealth.

What kind of King was this anyway?

The King who needed nothing.

The Ruler who was content simply to do the will of the Father.

The Potentate who defeated the world using only the weapons of love and truth.

Our Brother who took a nail in the hand for us; our Friend who took a spear in the side for us. All that we might be free. And content in Him.

THE SERMON ON THE MOUNT

Jesus' words in the Sermon on the Mount comprise the most powerful and influential discourse ever delivered in speech or writing. Thomas Jefferson's Declaration of Independence cannot compete, nor Lincoln's Gettysburg Address, nor Shakespeare in *Hamlet*, nor Martin Luther King's "I Have a Dream." No speech has been as frequently quoted, no sermon as much pondered.

Jesus did not *need* help with the Sermon on the Mount. He did not need help in crafting the words nor editorial help with revisions. He did not need to consult focus groups. He did not need notes or an outline. He did not need a stenographer to be sure it was all recorded accurately.

Jesus did not need these things to give the sermon because He was the sermon. The Sermon on the Mount was not so much what He said as who He was.

Here, again, is our totally different human. He looked like us, but make no mistake, He was not us. When He spoke, the universe held its breath and history changed its course.

Jesus' words on the Mount were like a prairie fire. Nothing was safe, nothing untouched. He scorched the landscape, wounded traditions, inverted power structures, annoyed a lot of people, and stood the world on its head. It was a consuming fire, but Jesus was not an arsonist. He needed to demolish the landscape so that a new kind of faith might grow in its place.

Bishop Gore said the Sermon on the Mount "was spoken into the ear of the Church and overhead by the world." John Stott said, "It is the nearest thing to a manifesto that he ever uttered, for it is his own description of what he wanted his followers to be and to do." C. S. Lewis responded to criticism that he seemed not to care for it: "As for 'caring for the Sermon on the Mount,' if 'caring for' here means 'liking' or enjoying, I suppose no one 'cares for' it. Who can like being knocked flat on his face by a sledge hammer? I can hardly imagine a more deadly spiritual condition than that of a man who can read that passage with tranquil pleasure."[20]

Want to know what keeps me up at night? What if Jesus actually meant all those radical things He said in the Sermon on the Mount?

BEATITUDES

Jesus begins the Sermon on the Mount full throttle, going 60 mph right out of the driveway. The Beatitudes are not a prelude to a symphony but a climax right at the start.

> Blessed are the poor in spirit,
>   for theirs is the kingdom of heaven.
> Blessed are those who mourn,
>   for they will be comforted.
> Blessed are the meek,
>   for they will inherit the earth.
> Blessed are those who hunger and thirst for righteousness,
>   for they will be filled.
> Blessed are the merciful,

for they will be shown mercy.
Blessed are the pure in heart,
    for they will see God.
Blessed are the peacemakers,
    for they will be called children of God.
Blessed are those who are persecuted because of righteousness,
    for theirs is the kingdom of heaven.[21]

In our first reading of the Beatitudes, we think how marvelous it is that Jesus would speak such kind and encouraging words to the suffering, misunderstood, the passed-over. He intentionally elevates an afflicted and overlooked class of people: the poor in spirit, those who mourn, the meek, those who hunger and thirst for righteousness, the merciful, the pure in heart, the peacemakers, and those who are persecuted because of righteousness. You will be comforted, He says, filled, set free, and rewarded.

We like to view ourselves as magnanimous like Jesus, on the side of the underdog, rooting for justice. It is therefore easy to come alongside such stepped-on people and wish them blessings. Sympathy rises easily for the undistinguished, unpromoted, unheralded, and uncelebrated. It's nice they can have this moment in the sun.

On second reading, after our magnanimity has been expressed and we feel better about ourselves, we breathe a sigh of relief that at least we are not included in this lineup. What a load of grief Jesus is addressing here—glad that's not me. Can you imagine this being your list of goals to accomplish in the next decade?

On third reading, we see that Jesus is speaking to us after all. If we are His disciples, living according to His words and example, these are the things we can look forward to. This list is precisely what the normal Christian life looks like in its matured state, which is why Carl F. Henry wrote, "Jesus clothes the beatitudes with His own life."

On fourth reading, we wonder how Jesus is going to pull this off. If we subject ourselves, as disciples of Christ, to the kingdom of God and His righteousness and this is what happens, how is He going to make the first half of each verse turn into the second half?

Answer: The Beatitudes came to life as soon as Jesus uttered them. His words became active the minute they escaped His mouth. They are now the law of eternity. If the first half of the verse describes us, the second half is automatic. He is the power behind these promises, and Jesus does not make idle promises. Everything He says He will do, He does. Everything He says will happen, happens. In fulfilling His promises in the Beatitudes, He brings to bear the same power that created the universe, redeemed it, sustains it, and will judge it.

It is important to note that Jesus is on the side of those He blesses here. They are His kind of people. It is obvious throughout His ministry that He has a preferential regard for the weak, the oppressed, and the poor, the kind of people who have few advantages in this world and few possessions. And that is a signal to us all.

Thascius would not have qualified for any portion of Jesus' words in the Beatitudes. Born in AD 200 to a well-placed family of Carthage, he was classically educated, wealthy, a lawyer, an orator, and a pagan. Then everything changed. After coming to faith at age forty-five, he changed his name to Cyprian, gave a goodly portion of his wealth to the poor, and wrote his intimate friend Donatus:

> This is a cheerful world as I see it from my garden under the shadows of my vines. But if I were to ascend some high mountain and look out over the wide lands, you know very well what I should see: brigands on the highways, pirates on the sea, armies fighting, cities burning; in the amphitheaters men murdered to please applauding crowds; selfishness and cruelty and misery and despair under all roofs. It is a bad world, Donatus, an incredibly bad world. But I have discovered in the midst of it a quiet and holy people who have learned a great secret. They have found a joy which is a thousand times better than any pleasure of our sinful life. They are despised and persecuted, but they care not. They are masters of their souls. They have overcome the world. These people, Donatus, are the Christians—and I am one of them.

Cyprian was baptized, became a church leader, suffered under two persecutions, and was decapitated by the Romans at age fifty-eight. Saying "thanks be to God," he went content to the swordsman, knowing he was numbered among Jesus' "Blessed are those . . ."

DO NOT WORRY

Jesus lived in a lofty disregard for status and possessions. He was content to trust the Father for His daily needs and steadfastly refused to worry. He told us, too, to stop worrying—the Father knows what we need as well.

Fast-forward to the twenty-first century, where worry is in an inflationary cycle. Despite more progress, privilege, and possessions than ever before, we are worried all the time. It seems that these advantages have only served to increase anxiety in every direction. The more we have, the more we worry. Why? Because we have more to lose. And that makes us fret.

So, bypassing Jesus' words, we take matters into our own hands. Since our stash is infinitely greater than in the time of Jesus, it is impractical for us to consider the Sermon on the Mount as even partially helpful. Modern economics and expectations have risen so high that it is hard to take Jesus seriously any longer. As a consequence, we use up much of our lives trying to insulate ourselves against insecurities. We work harder, buy more, accumulate, set aside, save, hoard, buy locks and security systems, maximize insurance—and much of this activity is driven by worry, anxiety, and a relentless discontent.

A string of ten verses in the Sermon on the Mount is directed at our day-to-day worries. Six times in these ten verses Jesus tells us that worry is useless, if not actually sinful.

> Therefore I tell you, do not *worry* about your life, what you will eat or drink; or about your body, what you will wear. Is not life more than food, and the body more than clothes? Look at the birds of the air; they do not sow or reap or store away in barns, and yet your heavenly

Father feeds them. Are you not much more valuable than they? Can any one of you by *worrying* add a single hour to your life?

And why do you *worry* about clothes? See how the flowers of the field grow. They do not labor or spin. Yet I tell you that not even Solomon in all his splendor was dressed like one of these. If that is how God clothes the grass of the field, which is here today and tomorrow is thrown into the fire, will he not much more clothe you — you of little faith? So do not *worry*, saying, "What shall we eat?" or "What shall we drink?" or "What shall we wear?" For the pagans run after all these things, and your heavenly Father knows that you need them. But seek first his kingdom and his righteousness, and all these things will be given to you as well. Therefore do not *worry* about tomorrow, for tomorrow will *worry* about itself. Each day has enough trouble of its own.[22]

Don't worry, six times. One wonders how many more times Jesus needs to say it. Even though He clearly tells us *do not worry about tomorrow*, I know hundreds of people who have absolutely no intention of giving up their worry.

Jesus knew that worrying was a profound waste. "Who of you by worrying can add a single hour to his life?" Worry does not add an hour to life, but it surely does subtract an hour. People who worry more, die younger. Now there's something to worry about. Worry does not improve tomorrow, it only poisons today. We do not solve any of our problems or insecurities by worrying about them.

Notice that Jesus does not tell us to ignore problems. It is perfectly acceptable to make plans to address difficulties, but it is not acceptable to worry about them. Worry is of no positive value. It does not take away our problems. It only takes away our peace, our rest, and our contentment. Perhaps worst of all, it distances us from Jesus because we regard His plan as no longer trustworthy. You think He doesn't notice?

Let me offer an example. I fly a fair amount, and on a normal day, it is eighty minutes through western Wisconsin to the Minneapolis airport. If I suspect bad weather, busy traffic, or road construction, it is appropriate for me to be concerned about these issues and to take steps to address my concerns. So I check the weather, monitor the construction site on the Internet, or leave earlier as needed. But once I'm on the road, it is silly for me to "worry" about catching my flight. I am not going to drive 90 mph. I cannot do anything about bumper-to-bumper traffic. I refuse to behave recklessly in a snowstorm. There's nothing to do but just keep driving until I reach the parking garage. Still, about 20 percent of the time, I worry. *The "margin guy" can't miss a flight.* How many flights, out of hundreds, have I missed? Not one. Worry does not help me arrive on time, but it is toxic to my body, mind, and spirit. I always pay a price, and that is a foolish way to start a trip.

Worry is the dysfunctional part of concern, just as hurry is the dysfunctional part of speed. It is okay to go fast, as long as we don't hurry, and it is okay to have concern, as long as we don't worry.

A subtheme of Jesus' life is an absence of worry for those who trust Him. Worry, fear, and anxiety are foreign concepts in His theology. Worry, fear, and anxiety are also driving engines for discontented living.

Know what we should probably worry about? In these particular ten verses, where Jesus says, "Seek *first* the kingdom of God and His righteousness," what if He wasn't kidding?

I WILL GIVE YOU REST

Let's visit a few other gospel passages where Jesus reaches out to our discontent. In Matthew 11:28, He presents us a marvelous gift. "Come to me, all you who are weary and burdened, and I will give you rest." This is quite an offer. When someone of this caliber is generous enough to offer a gift of this quality, it is wise to accept.

True restedness is a rare commodity today. We don't value it and feel guilty if we have it. None of our friends are rested and besides, there is far too much on our plates. Perhaps that is why Jesus expands the discussion. As part of His offer for rest, we are to share His yoke, learn from Him, find that He is gentle and humble in heart, that His yoke is easy and His burden is light. Then we will find rest for our souls. This just keeps getting better.

It is interesting to note that rest seldom travels alone. Contentment is a frequent companion, as are peace and absence of worry. Discontented people, on the other hand, almost never find "rest for their souls."

When Jesus extends this invitation, how complete is the rest He offers? Ten percent? Fifty percent? Eighty percent? Think about it. The rest Jesus offers is complete. If Jesus offers something, He must have both the power and authority to back it up. Jesus delivers on His side. Always.

When we understand the depth of what Jesus is expressing here, we know His rest can exceed any situation or suffering. Should we continue to be restless, we must not blame the Savior. He has made complete provision, and it is available to all believers regardless of their circumstances.

BEWARE COVETOUSNESS

His entire life, Jesus coveted nothing. Neither did He have a moment of discontent regarding possessions. Make no mistake, Jesus often exhibited a divine discontent regarding the spiritual status quo—but never regarding material things.

The word *covet* has a range of associated meanings, all negative in a biblical sense. On the milder side, to covet something means an excessive or extreme desire for that thing, which often leads to foolish actions, bad judgment, excessive debt, and moral lapses. On the more extreme side, to covet means wanting what your neighbor or another acquaintance has, even to the point of stealing it or perhaps wishing they didn't have it so you would feel better. This extends, ominously, to your neighbor's spouse.

As we shall see in the next chapter, to covet something was an instantly identifiable sin to the Jewish listener because it directly violated the Ten Commandments. The last commandment of the Decalogue forbids coveting your neighbor's, well, anything.[23]

In Luke 12, some family members came to Jesus asking for a settlement of an inheritance issue between them. Instead, He gives a now famous warning: "Take care, and be on your guard against all covetousness, for one's life does not consist in the abundance of his possessions."

Thus begins a parable about a rich land owner who had good land and bountiful crops. The farmer fantasized a grand scheme to tear down his barns and build even larger ones, storing all his grain and goods so in the end, he could relax, eat, drink, and be merry. Jesus continues: "But God said to him, 'Fool! This night your soul is required of you, and the things you have prepared, whose will they be?' So is the one who lays up treasure for himself and is not rich toward God."[24]

This story is not so much a firm statement against wealth as it is a warning against covetousness, or discontentment, for they are usually interconnected. The fully contented person, however, is guaranteed by definition to be someone who does not covet.

"Do not store up for yourselves treasures on earth," Jesus said in the Sermon on the Mount, "but store up for yourselves treasures in heaven."[25] Throughout His entire ministry, Jesus was consistent on the theme of money — that it is dangerous, it can harden our hearts against God, and it can lead to discontentment. Since the thrust of His entire message was freedom, it is easy to see why He so consistently steered us in the direction of contentment.

THE HOLY OF HOLIES IN SCRIPTURE

Chapters 13–17 of John have been called the Holy of Holies of the Bible, and for many years this has been my favorite section of Scripture. I have lived in these verses and have been thoroughly captivated. Allow me to explain.

Despite the MD after my name, my calling from God is to be a watchman on the wall, a discerner of the times, or, in more secular terms, a futurist. Though I have been engaged in this since 1982, I left medicine in 1996 to stand on the ramparts full time. For some this might seem strange, but the pull and the timing were undeniably clear. My leaving medicine was not related to problems or failure. In fact, I was successful in both private practice and academic medicine, loved my patients, won some awards, and have never been sued. But God had other plans for my life: to set up a diagnostic clinic at the edge of the globe and watch the nations spin past. My job is to examine the endless stream of data ("symptoms") coming over the horizon and attempt to make accurate diagnoses about what it all means. It is an intellectual feast of the first order, in a frightening sort of way.

In mid-2006, I noticed something strange happening, a global shaking. It has continued and is accompanied by high levels of volatility, dysfunctional math, destabilizing change, and soft-anarchy. As it turns out, we live in an unprecedented age, a special moment in history, and by my calculations, easily the most interesting time in the past 2,000 years.

That brings us back to the passage in John. Two millennia ago, Jesus was sitting with His disciples in the Upper Room, talking with them and preparing them. He knew what they did not, that their leaving these chambers would begin the worst twenty-four hours in the history of the universe. In that span of time, we would do the unthinkable — betray, arrest, abuse, accuse, scorn, prosecute, condemn, torture, and then crucify Jesus Christ, the Son of the Living God and Savior of the world.

Killing God is a very serious offense. Under normal circumstances, this would immediately be followed by the annihilation of the entire human race. Yet instead of a rising anger, Jesus was concerned about His friends and spoke to them in reassuring terms about love, joy, and peace. Can you imagine this? Love, joy, and peace? Really? The transcendence He displays here is incomprehensible. We simply are not a deep enough people to understand the magnitude of this demeanor. Even later, when He climbed back out of the grave, He still wasn't mad.

Then it hit me — Jesus is not speaking only to them but to us as well. We, too, live in a historic time, an epic era. Having first careened around the bend into uncharted territory, next we exploded off the tracks. The world system is now caught in an acceleration trap; we're headed straight up and can't figure a way out. Otherwise intelligent leaders are making it up as they go along. But if the world is pregnant on our generational shift, God knew all about it and granted us the privilege of encouraging the weak, nursing the wounded, and warning the wicked.

Remembering that Jesus has been here before, let's buckle our seat belts and listen to what He tells His yet unsuspecting disciples. In John 14:1, He tells them to calm their hearts, that they should not be troubled. He repeats the exact phrase again in verse 27. Think of it: Jesus is about to be beaten and slaughtered, but *He* tells *them* not to be troubled. Next, He announces that He is leaving but that it's okay. He is going to prepare a place for us, then will come back to get us so we can be together. He continues to speak repeatedly not only about love, joy, and peace, but also about truth, abiding in Him, bearing fruit, obeying, serving, asking and receiving, absence of fear, no longer servants but friends, and perhaps best of all, the soon arrival of the Spirit of truth, the Comforter, the Counselor.

Jesus is facing the worst, yet He thinks of us. There is no vengeance on His mind but instead glorification, love, and peace. He prays for the church, for all who come after, that we might have perfect unity, protection, and sanctification in the Word.

I am constrained by Jesus' remarkable performance in these chapters to trust Him fully and Him alone. Did He not say "apart from me you can do nothing"?[26] Yet how can I possibly take such an all-out stance without a perfect contentment in His leadership and provision?

We leave these remarkable chapters remembering that the disciples were troubled and that we too are troubled. But Jesus intends something better. He knows that in the next afternoon when He breathes His last, the sun will darken, the earth will tremble, the rocks will split, the tombs will open, the curtain will tear, and the disciples will flee. But He intends to have the last word: peace.

Peace I leave with you; my peace I give you. I do not give to you as the world gives. Do not let your hearts be troubled and do not be afraid.[27]

I have told you these things, so that in me you may have peace. In this world you will have trouble. But take heart! I have overcome the world.[28]

WHY DO YOU CALL ME LORD?

As we close this chapter, let us take one final look at a statement from Jesus. Actually, a question.

"Why do you call me, 'Lord, Lord,' and do not do what I say?"[29]

It is a good question. But, on second thought, wait a minute here. This perhaps deserves some push back. Why don't we do the things you say, Jesus? Well, have you ever listened to yourself? You are totally over the top on just about everything. Unrealistic is a word that comes to mind. Idealistic. Impractical. Impossible. And that's just for starters. We'll be marginalized. Our friends will think we're weird. People will snicker. Nobody acts like that New Testament stuff anymore.

But then we turn to 1 John 5:3 and read, "This is love for God: to keep his commands. And *his commands are not burdensome*" (emphasis added).

Oh.

CHAPTER 3

CONTENTMENT IN HISTORY

Seated in the Place of Honor

Fortify yourself with contentment, for this is an impregnable fortress.
— EPICTETUS, GREEK STOIC PHILOSOPHER

The Basel cathedral sits high over the Rhine, looking every bit the fourteenth-century spiritual fortress that it is. Each evening I would listen for the Münster's ten o'clock bells, then pad across the room to look at the stately structure from my third-story window. It was a perfect view from across the river: the Rhine flowing quietly to the German and French borders just a few miles away, and the lighted Münster standing guard. In the morning, after yogurt, bread, and hot milk with my Swiss family, the Vischers, I would cross the bridge on my way to the Study Center and greet the cathedral, "Guten Morgen," with a wave of the hand.

Night and day, for ten months, I watched the red sandstone sentinel. One might expect I had all details well memorized, and indeed I did. Except for one part—a tiny three-foot angel on the roof. It is not as if the little guy were hiding. On the contrary, he was very prominent, occupying the best perch in the canton looking directly down on the river far below. Somehow, though, I failed to notice.

Thirty years later, in 2002, our family's visit to Basel coincided with a gala affair. "Everyone is talking about it," the Vischers said. Some loved it; some hated it. The city had commissioned a Japanese artist to give the angel a temporary new home. If you wished to commune with the new celebrity, now it was easy. Just climb the narrow winding cathedral stairs to the roof, then scale a frightening, multi-angled scaffolding to his new one-room apartment 130 feet above the ground. Once there, knock, enter, and take a seat on the sofa. After centuries with no one to visit, the patient angel was in the middle of the room, waiting to greet all comers. I like to think he was smiling, perhaps having recognized me.

LIFTED HIGH

Our contentment angel is like that. Sitting high atop the church, all alone, watching over our lives as though to protect us from the bondage of discontent: greed, excess, envy, comparison, bitterness, unhappiness, strife, isolation, debt, ruin, and enmity with God. Despite such noble and persistent vigilance, however, our angel today is even lonelier than his Basel counterpart. Few of us notice him. Few want to climb the heights to sit, to commune, to seek counsel.

Part of the reason, obviously, is that we are too busy. We have no time for a hike up the stairs, let alone a climb up the mountain. Perhaps even more pertinent, we are no longer interested. We are headed down another road in a different direction. Contentment is a relic these days, and the angel's advice is not to be trusted. Listen to contentment and you lose. Those rushing headlong are convinced by the momentum of the crowd. The stampede is strong and self-confident. No one even whispers the angel's sweet name. Yet caution is in order, for this angel has the ear of God.

It is important to note that our modern anti-contentment attitude is out of the mainstream of history. Contentment has long been a principle in good standing, endorsed by philosophers, statesmen, men of letters, and theologians of all religions. Even if times were marked by destitution, tragedy, drought, war, famine, and pestilence; even if gutters were filled with beggars, doorways filled with prostitutes, and people beat each other with chickens; still, contentment was lifted high. Thought leaders endorsed contentment as a source of hidden bliss and riches, treasured within a human heart despite circumstances.

It is only recently, then, that contentment has fallen on hard times. With the arrival of progress and modern economics, something had to give, so finally contentment was pushed aside, trampled over, replaced by unbridled ambition. No one stopped to have a memorial service nor slowed to light a candle.

Although all humanity can benefit from the contentment doctrine (rightly interpreted, of course), those in the household of faith have a much stronger pull than the endorsement of history. We have the endorsement of God Himself, for the Scriptures leave us little choice but to act reverently toward contentment. Prominent are these four reasons:

1. The Tenth Commandment demands that we not covet.
2. The Wisdom Literature of the Old Testament, particularly Psalms and Proverbs, speaks eloquently of a calm satisfaction in God, His sovereignty, and His gifts.
3. The life and teachings of Jesus, as we have seen, reveal a consistent endorsement of contentment.
4. The Epistles contain three compelling passages where contentment is both commended and commanded: Philippians 4; 1 Timothy 6; and Hebrews 13.

Most of this book will be given to the discussion and application of these biblical positions. This chapter, however, will examine contentment in the broader sweep of time. While the majority of the references below speak of contentment with regard to the Judeo-Christian tradition, the list also includes literary, cultural, political, educational, and intellectual leaders in many settings. The point: Contentment was a virtue widely acknowledged and with broad support throughout history.

THE ERA OF WISDOM LITERATURE (~1,000 BC, WITH JOB MUCH EARLIER)

The five books of Wisdom Literature—Job, Psalms, Proverbs, Ecclesiastes, and Song of Songs—are much loved. They are ancient yet timeless. Each book makes its own significant contribution to contentment, but Psalms and Proverbs contain perhaps the most important endorsements.

The lyrical King David wrote half of the Psalms across a lengthy span of his life. He was a natural-born leader and fighter but also a poet, musician, and worshipper. We have already seen contentment expressed in Psalm 23, "The LORD is my shepherd, I lack nothing." David consistently made a habit of expressing his surrender to the sufficiency of the Almighty. "My heart is not proud, LORD, my eyes are not haughty; I do not concern myself with great matters or things too wonderful for me. But I have calmed and quieted myself; I am like a weaned child with its mother."[1] Another version reads, "I have kept my soul calm and quiet. My soul is content as a weaned child is content in its mother's arms."[2] This is not the usual image cultivated by a feared king over a large empire, but David did not really care about such things. His focus was on God.

Asaph, David's musical director, wrote twelve of the Psalms. In Psalm 73, he confesses to seeing the prosperity of another and envying it—the very picture of discontent. Yet, in the end, he did not falter.

> But as for me, my feet had almost slipped;
>   I had nearly lost my foothold.
> For I envied the arrogant
>   when I saw the prosperity of the wicked. . . .

> Yet I am always with you;
>   you hold me by my right hand.
> You guide me with your counsel,
>   and afterward you will take me into glory.
> Whom have I in heaven but you?
>   And earth has nothing I desire besides you.[3]

Proverbs is a much-revered source of wisdom and counsel, and some read from it on a daily basis. Wish to rest content? "The fear of the LORD leads to life; then one rests content, untouched by trouble."[4] In another chapter, Solomon, despite his riches, writes, "Give me neither poverty nor riches, but give me only my daily bread. Otherwise, I may have too much and disown you and say, 'Who is the LORD?' Or I may become poor and steal, and so dishonor the name of my God."[5] Notice he was advocating neither affluence nor asceticism, but instead the kind of moderation found in contentment.

Outside the Wisdom Literature, one of my favorite Old Testament passages comes from Habakkuk. As the book opens, the prophet is challenging God's judgments. By the end, however, he yields completely even if surrounded by suffering. "Though the fig tree does not bud and there are no grapes on the vines, though the olive crop fails and the fields produce no food, though there are no sheep in the pen and no cattle in the stalls, yet I will rejoice in the LORD, I will be joyful in God my Savior. The Sovereign LORD is my strength."[6] It is a sign of the deepest maturity to exhibit such contentment in extreme circumstances.

GREEK AND ROMAN (CLASSICAL ANTIQUITY) ERA (800 BC–AD 500)

The Greeks and Romans did not have the benefit of reading the Wisdom Literature—they developed an appreciation of contentment on their own. Philosophers were enormously influential in the Classical Era. Socrates (470–399 BC) was followed by his prize student, Plato (424–348 BC), who in turn was followed by his prize student, Aristotle (384–322 BC). This "Athenian school" of philosophy became a reference point for all that followed.

Socrates famously said, "Contentment is natural wealth; luxury, artificial poverty." At another time, "He is richest who is content with the least; for contentment is the wealth of nature." Plato followed with a similar theme, "The greatest wealth is to live content with little."

Following the passing of this famous trio, the two main schools of philosophy were Epicureanism and Stoicism. Both sought contented living. The epicureans believed that a happy life was attained through calm, tranquil, and moderate pleasures, especially physical health, peace of mind, prudence, and friendship. (Its reputation for rampant hedonism is not deserved.) Epicurus (341–270 BC), the Greek founder of Epicurean philosophy, said, "Do not spoil what you have by desiring what you have not; remember that what you now have was once among the things you only hoped for." Several centuries later, Horace (65–8 BC), a Roman Epicurean philosopher, poet, and satirist, wrote, "You traverse the world in search of happiness, which is within the reach of every man; a contented mind confers it on all." Also, "Let him who has enough ask for nothing more."

The stoics believed that a sage should not suffer destructive emotions but should instead exhibit behaviors that cultivated virtue and the greatest good. At the extreme end, they maintained that a single olive per day would be enough to sustain oneself. Seneca (4 BC–AD 65), Roman stoic philosopher, statesman, and playwright, sounded like the apostle Paul in Philippians 4 when he wrote, "Happy the man who can endure the highest and the lowest fortune. He who has endured such vicissitudes with equanimity, has deprived misfortune of its power." Epictetus (AD 55–135), Greek stoic philosopher, wrote, "He is a wise man who does not grieve for the things which he has not, but rejoices for those which he has." Marcus Aurelius (AD 121–180), Roman emperor and stoic philosopher, wrote, "Very little is needed to make a happy life."

POST-CLASSICAL ERA: DARK AGES AND MIDDLE AGES (AD 500–1500)

Following the collapse of the Roman Empire in 476, much of the Western world lapsed into an unspectacular melancholic millennium of undistinguished muddling. Feudalism, the Crusades, and the inquisitions were occasionally brightened by such developments as the Magna Carta in 1215. There were so few voices of note during this thousand years that we can perhaps be excused for dipping back a century to hear from the great Augustine (AD 354–430). This brilliant Christian philosopher and theologian wrote, "As for me, I know no other contentment but clinging to God, because unless my being remains in Him, it cannot remain in me." In one of his most famous passages, he said, "The thought of you stirs him so deeply that he cannot be content unless he praises you, because you made us for yourself and our hearts find no peace until they rest in you."

Bernard of Clairvaux (1090–1153) was a French abbot, theologian, and hymnist. Martin Luther said he was the best monk who ever lived, "whom I admire beyond all the rest put together." Perhaps typical of most monks, he wrote, "Let your prayer for temporal blessings be strictly limited to things absolutely necessary." Thomas à Kempis (1380–1471), famous for writing *The Imitation of Christ*, was a German priest, monk, and copyist of the Bible. "May I seek my repose in You above everything that is not You, my God. For my heart cannot rest or be fully content until, rising above all gifts and every created thing, it rests in You."

THE EARLY MODERN ERA (1500–1750)

The early modern era began with the fall of Constantinople in 1453. It was driven, in succession, by the invention of the printing press, the European Renaissance, the discovery of the New World, the Reformation, and the Age of Enlightenment. After a prolonged period of stagnancy, change began to accelerate. In the midst of this new dynamic, voices of faith taught the principle of contentment as important to Scripture and honoring to God.

The highest art, said Martin Luther (1483–1546), is to "be content with the calling in which God has placed you." Others taught we should be content with our "lot" in life. William Ames (1576–1633), an English clergy and philosopher, wrote, "The virtue of contentment is the acquiescence of the mind in the lot God has given." The brilliant and often hard-to-read theologian John Owen (1616–1683) agreed. "Learn to be contented with your lot. Our wise God gave you exactly what is commensurate for your good."

Two church leaders, Jeremiah Burroughs (1599–1646) and Thomas Watson (1620–1686), published excellent books on the topic. Burroughs wrote in *The Rare Jewel of Christian Contentment*, "Christian contentment is that sweet, inward, quiet, gracious frame of spirit, which freely submits to and delights in God's wise and fatherly disposal in every condition." Watson followed with *The Art of Divine Contentment*. "Discontent doth dislocate and unjoint the soul, it pulls off the wheels. . . . Discontent is a fretting humour, which dries the brains, wastes the spirits, corrodes and eats out the comfort of life. . . . Why do you complain of your troubles? It is not trouble that troubles, but discontent."

Samuel Rutherford (1600–1661), the Scottish Presbyterian theologian, was so esteemed that Charles Spurgeon said his letters were "the nearest thing to inspiration which can be found in all the writings of mere men." Despite the death of his family, Rutherford wrote, "Think it not hard if you get not your will, nor your delights in this life; God will have you to rejoice in nothing but himself." Thomas Jacombe (1622–1687), a contemporary, wrote, "When a man likes whatsoever God doeth *to* him or *with* him . . . this is contentment. . . . Whatever pleases Him pleaseth me, be it imprisonment, poverty, sickness, reproach, death itself. Let God's will be done, and I am content."

George Herbert (1593–1633), one of my favorite poets, said, "A wise man cares not for what he cannot have." Isaac Watts (1674–1748), one of my favorite hymn writers, wrote, "I would not change my blest estate for all the world calls good or great." Matthew Henry (1662–1714), one of my favorite commentators, said, "The more we accommodate ourselves to plain things, and the less we indulge in those artificial delights which gratify pride and luxury, the nearer we approach to a state of innocency." John Bunyan (1628–1688), one of the world's favorite authors, wrote in *Pilgrim's Progress*:

He that is down need fear no fall, He that is low no pride.

He that is humble ever shall have God to be his guide.

I am content with what I have, Little be it, or much.

And, Lord! Contentment still I crave, Because Thou savest such.

This is the "Song of the Shepherd Boy in the Valley of Humiliation." Some might recognize it also as the song sung by Beth in Louisa May Alcott's *Little Women,* sickly though she was and soon to die.

We cross the Atlantic to hear our last couple of voices. The eminent preacher and theologian, Jonathan Edwards (1703–1758), definitively wrote, "There is provision in Christ for the satisfaction and full contentment of the needy and thirsty soul." At one point, Edwards housed a guest, David Brainerd (1718–1747), the young zealous missionary to Native Americans. After he had fallen ill among the Indians, Brainerd wrote, "I am in a very poor state of health; but through Divine goodness, I am not discontented. I bless God for this retirement! I never was more thankful for anything than I have been of late for the necessity I am under of self-denial in many respects." He came to stay with the Edwards family where he was affectionately nursed by their seventeen-year-old daughter, Jerusha. Brainerd died of tuberculosis six months later at the age of twenty-nine. Four months following, Jerusha became ill with TB and died in five days. The two are buried side by side. Far from being spiteful, Edwards wrote *The Life of David Brainerd,* which became his best-selling work and challenged many generations of future missionaries.

THE EARLY MODERN ERA (SECULAR VOICES)

There were corresponding secular voices speaking of contentment at the same time. Sir Philip Sidney (1554–1586), the English poet and courtier, wrote, "The highest point outward things can bring unto is the contentment of the mind; with which no estate can be poor, without which all estates will be miserable." Compare this to a contemporary,

Robert Greene (1560–1592), England's first professional writer and dramatist: "A mind content both crown and kingdom is." Both speak of contentment in our thought life. Sidney died of a battle wound at age thirty-one; Greene died at age thirty-two.

Greene is given credit for the first writing that refers to Shakespeare (1564–1616), criticizing him for trying to be both actor and writer. Yet they wrote similarly how contentment prefers the lower classes over kings and princes, and they did it in similar style. Greene wrote, "Such sweet content, such minds, such sleep, such bliss; Beggars enjoy, which princes often do miss." Shakespeare, just beginning his career when Greene died, wrote in *Henry VI*,

My crown is in my heart, not on my head,
Nor decked with diamonds and Indian stones,
Nor to be seen: my crown is called content:
A crown it is, that seldom kings enjoy.

Two Frenchmen wrote with a touch of irony and satire regarding contentment but in a manner helpful to our discussion. François Duc de La Rochefoucauld (1613–1680), a writer and nobleman, suggested, "Before we set our hearts too much on anything, let us examine how happy are those who already possess it." Jean de La Bruyère (1645–1696) was an essayist and moralist who spent a great deal of time at court and then wrote disparagingly about his observations. "If you carefully observe people incapable of praise, who always blame, who are never contented with anyone, you will recognize that these are the very people with whom no one else is content." A third Frenchman, the writer Vauvenargues (1715–1747), offered a heartening perspective on our topic. "We can console ourselves for not having great talents as we console ourselves for not having great places. We can be above both in our hearts." This, in short, is our quest.

Two brilliant contemporaries on opposite shores offered important teachings on contentment. Samuel Johnson (1709–1784) is regarded as arguably the most distinguished man of letters in English history.

He spoke of contentment as arising from our character and thought life. "The fountain of contentment must spring up in the mind, and they who have so little knowledge of human nature as to seek happiness by changing anything but their own disposition, will waste their lives in fruitless efforts and multiply the grief they propose to remove." Ben Franklin (1706–1790) was a multiply-gifted genius and a true Renaissance man: author, diplomat, inventor, physicist, politician, printer, newspaper owner—and that's only a partial list. He spoke of contentment, as have many, from the perspective of redefined riches. "Content makes poor men rich; discontentment makes rich men poor."

THE LATE MODERN ERA (1750 TO THE PRESENT)

This era witnesses the most explosive developments in human history. The Industrial Revolution, the American and French Revolutions, the rise of capitalism, technology, and modern health care—these are but part of the story to be explored in the next chapter. Rapid improvements on multiple fronts were often accompanied by disruptive change. Still, contentment remained in good standing as a widely accepted principle of theology and philosophy.

One obstacle to biblical contentment is submission to the will of God, an issue addressed by contemporaries William S. Plumer (1802–1880) and Harvey Newcomb (1803–1863), both American writers and clergy. Plumer wrote, "The difficulty therefore is not so much in the lack of good rules and strong reasons for guiding us into a state of contentment, as in the deep-rooted aversion of our hearts to a duty which requires our submission to the will of God." Newcomb continued with this theme: "The doctrine of a 'particular providence' is precious to the Christian's heart. It enables him to see the hand of God in every event. Hence the sinfulness of a repining, discontented, unsubmissive temper. It is difficult to reconcile the habitual indulgence of such a disposition with the existence of grace in the heart. The first emotion of the newborn soul is submission to the will of God."

Elsewhere, Newcomb wrote how contentment ties in with spiritual rest. "If God directs all our ways, and has promised to give us just what he sees we need, we surely ought to rest satisfied with what we have; for we know it is just what the Lord, in his infinite wisdom and unbounded goodness, sees fit to give us. It is, then, evidently the duty of every Christian to maintain a contented and cheerful spirit in all circumstances." J. R. Miller (1840–1912) picked up the same theme. "This is the true secret of Christian contentment, wherever it is found. We cannot make our own circumstances; we cannot keep away the sickness, the pain, the sorrow, the misfortune from our life; yet as Christians we are meant to live in any and all experiences in unbroken peace, in sweet restfulness of soul."

"Few, I am afraid, have the least idea what a shortcut to happiness it is to be content," wrote J. C. Ryle (1816–1900), English preacher and prolific writer. "To be content is to be rich and well off. He is the rich man who has no wants, and requires no more. I ask not what his income may be. A man may be rich in a cottage and poor in a palace." Henry Ward Beecher (1813–1887) agreed. "In this world, it is not what we take up, but what we give up, that makes us rich." George MacDonald (1824–1905), the Scottish author and minister who influenced C. S. Lewis perhaps more than any other writer, said, "I do not think that the road to contentment lies in despising what we have not got. Let us acknowledge all good, all delight that the world holds, and be content without it."

All of this works its way out through faith. Charles Kingsley (1819–1875), English priest, historian, and novelist, wrote, "We shall be made truly wise if we be made content; content, too, not only with what we can understand, but content with what we do not understand — the habit of mind which theologians call, and rightly, faith in God." This faith helps secure our contentment, understanding that God looks after our well-being and His own glory. Octavius Winslow (1808–1878), American preacher and descendant of *Mayflower*'s John Winslow, wrote, "Let this precious truth, 'My times are in your hand,' divest your mind of all needless, anxious care for the present or the future. . . .

Wherever you are placed, God has a work for you to do, a purpose through you to be accomplished, in which He blends your happiness with His Glory." Even when we don't understand why God has placed us in a situation, it is enough to trust through faith the Father's will. Hannah Whitall Smith (1832–1911) wrote, "If the Lord sets you to guard a lonely post in perfect stillness from all active work, you ought to be just as content as to be in the midst of the active warfare. It is no virtue to love the Master's work better than the Master's will." The American deaf-blind Helen Keller (1880–1968) is a striking example. "Everything has its wonders, even darkness and silence, and I learn, whatever state I may be in, therein to be content."

THE LATE MODERN ERA (SECULAR VOICES)

There are too many particulars and not enough space to include all the secular voices during this era, but room enough for some of the more interesting comments.

David Hume (1711–1776), the eminent Scottish philosopher, historian, and economist, wrote, "He is happy whose circumstances suit his temper; but he is more excellent who can suit his temper to any circumstances." A century later, William Gladstone (1809–1898), the unequaled four-time British Prime Minister, wrote, "Be happy with what you have and are, be generous with both, and you won't have to hunt for happiness."

Two giants of German intellectual thought were Immanuel Kant (1724–1804) and Johann Wolfgang von Goethe (1749–1832). The philosopher Kant wrote, "We are not rich by what we possess but by what we can do without." Goethe offered his *Nine Requisites for Contented Living*: "Health enough to make work a pleasure. Wealth enough to support your needs. Strength to battle with difficulties and overcome them. Grace enough to confess your sins and forsake them. Patience enough to toil until some good is accomplished. Charity enough to see some good in your neighbor. Love enough to move you to be useful and helpful to others. Faith enough to make real the things of God. Hope enough to remove all anxious fears concerning the future."

The transcendentalists, such as Ralph Waldo Emerson (1803–1882) and Henry David Thoreau (1817–1862), endorsed both simplicity and contentment. Emerson: "Can anything be so elegant as to have few wants, and to serve them one's self?" Thoreau: "Let your capital be simplicity and contentment." Also: "I am grateful for what I am and have. My thanksgiving is perpetual. It is surprising how contented one can be with nothing definite—only a sense of existence. My breath is sweet to me. O how I laugh when I think of my vague indefinite riches. No run on my bank can drain it, for my wealth is not possession but enjoyment."

Henri Frederic Amiel (1821–1881), Swiss writer, poet, and philosopher, wrote, "True humility is contentment." Marie von Ebner-Eschenbach (1830–1916), Austrian novelist, wrote, "To be content with little is difficult; to be content with much, impossible." Alfred Nobel (1833–1896), Swedish inventor of dynamite and founder of the Nobel Prize, wrote, "Contentment is the only real wealth."

Emily Dickinson (1830–1886), the much-loved, much-introverted American poet undiscovered in her time, had a gentle way with words. "Eden is that old-fashioned house we dwell in every day, without suspecting our abode until we drive away." Born fifty years later, American playwright Channing Pollock (1880–1946) said, "Happiness is a way station between too little and too much."

India's Mahatma Gandhi (1869–1948) taught, "Man falls from the pursuit of the ideal of plain living and high thinking the moment he wants to multiply his daily wants. Man's happiness really lies in contentment." All the major world religions seem to largely agree with Ghandi, including Buddhism, Hinduism, and Islam. It is quite astounding to find the near universal endorsement of contentment across the spectrum of faiths.

As we end this section, I wish to leave the reader with three contentment statements that summarize much of our current difficulty in this area. We will encounter each comment later in the text, but they are so succinctly stated and analytically accurate we would do well to consider them more than once.

> Give a man everything he desires and yet at this very moment he will feel that everything is not everything.
>
> IMMANUEL KANT (1724–1804), GERMAN PHILOSOPHER

> Man never has what he wants, because what he wants is everything.
>
> C. F. RAMUZ (1878–1947), FRENCH POET, ESSAYIST

> You say, "If I had a little more, I should be very satisfied." You make a mistake. If you are not content with what you have, you would not be satisfied if it were doubled.
>
> CHARLES SPURGEON (1834–1892), "PRINCE" OF BRITISH PREACHERS

BEATEN DOWN, REACHING UP

A high view of contentment was a consistent pattern across the ages. This, of course, does not mean that existence was easy and the streets filled with smiling citizens. Quite the opposite. Throughout most of history, life has been marked by tragedy and destitution. But when wealth and health were stripped away, when young children were dead and buried, when men and boys went off to war and returned home broken, there remained the possibility of *something inside* combining with *something above* to give hope. As unlikely as it sounds, peace and rest are possible amongst the ruins.

From China comes a man whose experience and words sound as if he has a contentment mindset from a previous century. Brother Yun was born in 1958 and became a Christian at age sixteen. He was deeply involved in the Chinese house church movement and, as a result, persecuted, beaten, and imprisoned repeatedly. After four imprisonments lasting seven years, he escaped prison and eventually fled the country only to be incarcerated again in Myanmar. The German embassy was able to secure his release after seven months, and that country today serves as Yun's base for worldwide ministry.

What is his attitude toward his afflictions?

> We never pray against our government or call down curses on them. Instead, we have learned that God is in control both of our own lives and the government we live under. . . . God has used China's government for his own purposes, molding and shaping his children as he sees fit. Instead of focusing our prayers against any political system, we pray that regardless of what happens to us, we will be pleasing to God.[7]

The gift of contentment says that striving is not inevitable. It is not a given that circumstances should rule our lives. Security is not ours alone to manage. Betrayal might be a fact, but bitterness is neither automatic nor compulsory. Pain is perhaps a daily reality but anger need not be. God controls all, including the margins. He has provided a way. We are not alone. Contentment in Him becomes our "harvest song of inward peace."

CHAPTER 4

THE MODERN DE-EMPHASIS OF CONTENTMENT

A Dangerous Neglect

To walk out of God's will is to walk into nowhere.

— C. S. LEWIS

A braham grew up among the Sumerians in modern-day Iraq around 2000 BC. He was Semitic and not of their stock—Ur of the Chaldeans was a thoroughly Sumerian city. It must have been an interesting place at an interesting time, for the Sumerians were mysteriously exceptional. They built canals, used extensive irrigation, improved roads, and established widespread commerce. Their ships ranged far. The farmers cultivated not only crops but herds and orchards. Their education required students to study from sunrise to sunset. Scholars developed the cuneiform script and the first systematized writing. They also created a system of arithmetic, geometry, and algebra, introduced the abacus, and mapped the stars. They divided a circle into sixty units, which later became the basis for our clocks. They developed a code of laws and also musical tunings still used today. They built impressive ziggurats, in some respects superior to the Egyptian pyramids. Where did they come from? Who knows. The wildest rumors have them dropping in from beyond the stars.

Then the Amorites sacked and burned the cities, and the Sumerian era ended.

The same happened with the Egyptians, Babylonians, Assyrians, Greeks, Romans, and scores of additional kingdoms. Up they soared, down they fell. An Egyptian pharaoh boasted, "Look upon my works, ye mighty, and despair." Then the sands blew in and covered him over.[1]

For purposes of comparison, let's fast-forward to the fourteenth century. Understand that this is a jump of 3.5 millennia, nearly equal to our traveling all the way back to the time of Christ and then returning home again. Historian Barbara Tuchman labels the 1300–1399 era "the calamitous century" that was "born to woe." Another historian said it was "a bad time for humanity." First came persistent cold weather, the "little Ice Age." Torrential rains followed, comparable to the biblical flood. Crops failed and famine spread across Europe. Millions died. The Hundred Years War between the English and the French began in 1337, devouring five generations. A decade later, beginning in 1347, the Black Death swept through. Bubonic plague killed one-third of the population from India to Norway, including as many as 60 percent of Europeans. The forgettable century was a time of massacres of Jews in pogroms, bad government, heresies, insurrections, horrors, brigandage, natural and man-made disasters, and schism in the church. Tuchman summarizes it as a "violent, tormented, bewildered, suffering and disintegrating age, a time, as many thought, of Satan triumphant."[2]

Now compare this "calamitous" record of fourteenth-century Europe with the accomplishments of the Sumerians 3,500 years earlier. To do so, suppose we engage in a thought experiment. First, we drop in on the Sumerians from a spaceship and live among their cities for a month. Later, we return to earth a second time and land in the Europe of 1350. What would be our impressions? The differences would appear nearly apocalyptic.

A full analysis of this comparison would require a separate book. Instead, I simply wish to ask a single generalized question from 30,000 feet: *What in the world went wrong?*

How is it possible to go so completely in reverse? After three and a half millennia, shouldn't things have gotten better rather than worse? Could not the world simply have built onto what was known by the Sumerians, then teach it forward and keep advancing? Add the best from the Babylonians, then the Egyptians, the Greeks, the Romans, and especially add the teachings of Christ, and just continue moving forward. That way, history would keep automatically advancing.

That's the phrase we've been waiting for, "automatically advancing." Want to know *"What in the world went wrong?"* There was no precedent for automatically advancing. In other words, they had no functioning sense of progress.

PROGRESS: A GIFT FROM GOD

Progress is a gift from God. He knew life would be tough, so He gave us many gifts to help, gifts such as water, plants, soil, the sun, creativity, eyes, a brain, a spirit, music, laughter, and relationships. Hundreds of gifts. Jesus, too, the greatest gift of Christmas long ago. The Spirit of Truth and Word of God as well. Progress, also, is a gift from God, and a powerful one.

What is *progress*? It is the notion that life automatically improves. Under the care and tutelage of progress, ten years into the future will automatically be better than the present. The same for thirty years and fifty years.

One mechanism progress uses to make life better is a reliable continuation of knowledge. In today's world, knowledge is always retained and multiplied. It is impossible for knowledge to disappear, and thus modern knowledge is irreversible. We cannot unlearn what has been learned, nor undiscover what has been discovered.

This, however, was not the case between the 2000 BC of Sumer and the AD 1350 of Europe. During this span, there was no guaranteed progress. There was no automatic trajectory of improvement. There was no assurance that knowledge would perpetuate. Every span of advancement was eventually matched by a span of regression. This did not particularly surprise our distant ancestors, because no one expected reliable improvement. It had never happened before, so why expect it now? Progress was a notion with no reference.

One way to illustrate this stagnancy across time is to look at life expectancy. The indicator of life expectancy is a good measure of a wide range of factors: income, education, understanding of hygiene, insight into the transmissibility of infectious disease, awareness of public health issues, access to clean water and safe food, and so on. The following table compares life expectancy over a four-thousand-year span.

Sumerian era	26 years
Greek & Roman era	28 years
Medieval England	30 years
England in the 1600s	35 years
U.S. in 1850	38 years
U.S. in 1900	48 years
U.S. today	>78 years

The earlier ancient numbers are low, partly because so many died in childhood. In addition, people died all across the age spectrum from complications of childbirth, infectious diseases, malnutrition, epidemics, accidents, and war.

Several observations are apparent. The first 3,500 years of this chart show minimal increase in overall life expectancy. Then, slowly, improvement came. By the 1600s in England, the figures begin to reflect modest gains. They inched even higher in the U.S. of 1850. In 1900, life expectancy jumped to forty-eight years. And during the twentieth and twenty-first centuries, it soared.

This mapping of life expectancy gives an accurate picture of the history of progress.

THREE ERAS OF PROGRESS

The history of progress can be divided into three periods, each having its own opinion of contentment. The first period lasted about 5,000 years, the second 250 years, and the third, 25 years. In terms of percentages, this gives the first era 95 percent of the time, the second era 4.5 percent, and the third era only 0.5 percent of the time. Though our slice of the pie is short, more has happened in our era than the first two eras combined. Incomprehensibly more.

Progress 1.0 — Slow, Grinding, and Destitute (3100 BC–AD 1750)

The first era of progress spans nearly 5,000 years, from the beginning of recorded history (Sumerian writings in 3100 BC) until the Industrial Revolution. In this era, progress was generally flat and unimpressive. The pitiable occupants of the fourteenth century were victims of this period and its paltry progress. So were nearly all residents across these five millennia. Yes, some empires were rich and powerful, but few inhabitants shared in the benefits of a bountiful life. Most lived close to the land where life was difficult, work was hard, taxes brutal, children died, and crops failed.

People in those days did not think about progress because there was nothing to think about. In the same way, I suppose, as I don't think about eating granite with gravy, living on the sun, or my Cubs winning the World Series. Progress was a nonissue, a fantasy, a fairy tale.

Contentment during this time, however, was a different story. As we have seen, Greek and Roman philosophers thought fondly of contentment, as did other reflective individuals. Those who obeyed the Scriptures and loved Christ had additional reasons to revere contentment even in the midst of afflictions. The esteemed Samuel Rutherford (1600–1661) lived during this time. Although he reached the age of sixty-one, he lost his first wife and also eight of his nine children at a young age. "Let your children be as so many flowers, borrowed from God," he said. "If the flowers die or wither, thank God for a summer loan of them." John Owen, a contemporary of Rutherford who lived to age sixty-seven, also was acquainted with grief. He lost ten of his eleven children in infancy. Yet he could say, "Learn to be contented with your lot. Our wise God gave you exactly what is commensurate for your good. Had He known that a foot's breadth more had been needful, you would have had it." Hardship and suffering often make the reality of contentment more precious.

Progress 2.0 — Ascendant, Glorious, and Hopeful (1750–2000)

The second era of progress began around 1750. Suddenly, the slumbering giant awoke. With the arrival of the Industrial Revolution and Enlightenment, progress gained traction, promptly took charge, and changed the world. It was a time of excitement, energy, and optimism.

How did progress accomplish so much so fast? Through a confluence of historic new developments. On the technology side, bubbling up among such yeasty conditions were the steam engine, power loom, cotton gin, electric motor, steamboat, locomotive, oil well, telegraph, telephone, lightbulb, diesel engine, wireless radio, dynamite, and airplane. On the sociopolitical side, changes were just as dramatic: liberty, democracy, self-governance, universal education, individual rights, tolerance, and the scientific method. Adam Smith turned economics into a science. Health care contributed general anesthesia, the germ theory of disease, vaccinations, and antibiotics. Larger ships set off for more distant ports, increasing commerce. The world was opening up, lives were improving, money was being made, and history was on the move.

With progress now steaming along on all cylinders, life was more hopeful. People developed a faith in progress and began to dream in optimistic terms about the future of their children and grandchildren. As for contentment, even among these burgeoning new conditions it was not forgotten. Jonathan Edwards, Ben Franklin, Samuel Johnson, Immanuel Kant, Goethe, Ralph Waldo Emerson, William Gladstone, Albert Nobel, Charles Spurgeon, Bertrand Russell, Helen Keller, and Karl Barth — all inhabitants of this period — put in a good word.

Progress 3.0 — Explosive, Uncontrollable, and Volatile (Past 25 Years)

We now arrive at the most interesting part of our story. Over this past quarter century, history suddenly exploded and threw us off our trajectory. We jumped the tracks and careened into the unknown. For better or worse, we find ourselves in the midst of an epic transition. The old patterns appear broken. The world is now a different place and is not playing by the rules.

Without warning, progress went vertical, heading straight for the stratosphere. We are locked in an *acceleration trap* and somehow can't escape. The entire globe seems to be making it up as we go along.

The math is now behaving strangely and no longer works in a variety of critical settings. The numbers are increasingly incomprehensible, the curves increasingly exponential (the profusion curve is actually hyperexponential), and the math increasingly dysfunctional (see the appendix, Dysfunctional Math, on page 211). As a result, nearly everything is being shaken — economics at personal, family, local, state, and federal levels; budget deficits; the stock and bond markets; the U.S. dollar; credit ratings; the middle class; real estate; higher education; elementary and secondary education; employment and job security; worker engagement; health care; bioethics; politics at state, federal, and global levels; the institution of family; energy and energy policy; demographics; immigration; publishing and all print media (books, magazines, newspapers); the music industry; the military and NATO; the auto and airline industries; entitlements such as Medicare, Medicaid, and Social Security; religion and denominations; traditions; farming; Europe; the Middle East; South Central Asia; Japan; China — and that's only a partial list. This accelerated level of change has been disruptive and destabilizing. Volatility is widespread, the new normal.

Profusion Graph, 3100 BC to AD 2000

Profusion is the generalized phenomenon of more — more and more of everything faster and faster — all added together into one number per year and graphed across history. This is an accurate graph, and it is *much more* than a simple population or economics graph. It is hyperexponential and is always underestimated.

This is not a time to doze off, for history is being made on our generational shift. It is a boiling, magnificent, stressful, fascinating, dangerous, unstable, exponential, overloaded, intense, complex, unstoppable vortex of swirling transition. Enormous amounts of change are now routinely seen in compressed time frames. By my observations, these changes have come so suddenly that not one in a thousand has a clear understanding of the mathematical drama we are facing.

To be sure, the world has witnessed almost continuous change to at least some degree — but never before with such levels of speed, suddenness, complexity, intensity, information, communication, media, money, mobility, technology, weaponry, and interconnectedness.

We have the honor of living in the most interesting time in the past 2,000 years. It is an emotional challenge, an intellectual feast, and a spiritual privilege.

BASSINETS TO BOMBS

Progress works, in essence, by giving us more and more of everything faster and faster. (There is much more to this discussion, but I will refer the reader to my earlier works on the topic.[3]) At first, progress languished in its role. No longer. Today, it puts on a dazzling show: a global economy of $70 trillion, space stations and artificial islands, buildings the size of small mountains, supertankers as large as castles, shopping malls with lakes inside, four million miles of paved roadways in the U.S. alone, satellites 200 miles high that can track a cat, a CERN particle accelerator generating one billion particle interactions per second and creating one trillion bytes of information per second, and computers so powerful that to equal it, "three-billion people using a pocket calculator would have to perform one million operations per second."[4]

Progress has been so astoundingly successful of late that it has assumed a dominant global role. Aside from spiritual realities, progress is now the most powerful force on the face of the earth.

The power of progress derives largely from the fact that it has taken control of the economic system in the West and increasingly the entire world. Since its recent successes exceeded anybody's wildest expectations, progress was awarded the keys to the kingdom. It is now in charge. It is no trivial matter to have a single process controlling the power of the world's economies.

Few realize just how completely we have relinquished control. Because the economy must continue to thrive at all costs, progress gets what it wants, when it wants it. This, in essence, makes progress autonomous. Even if this sounds alarming, there is no appeal. We do not tell progress what to do; progress tells us what to do. We feed it, and it gives us more. But feeding it is not a request, it is a command. We cannot tell progress when to slow or stop, and even if we could, such decelerations would be disastrous. Our economy would disintegrate, and damage to the economy is something that must never be allowed.

Progress uses a simple formula to generate success. It is a one-trick pony, a specialist. Its specialty is the four-letter word *more*, and its advertising slogan is "More and more of everything faster and faster." Progress does not care what kind of *more*—we can now choose from millions of goods and services, from bassinets to bombs, from penicillin to pornography—just as long as people are willing to pay for it.

First progress gives us . . .

more technology	more computers	more printers
more information	more televisions	more media
more news	more e-mail	more cell phones
more communication	more social media	more accessibility
more choices	more decisions	more activities
more commitments	more possessions	more expectations

Next progress gives us . . .

more multitasking	more debt	more work
more stress	more change	more complexity
more imbalance	more intensity	more overload
more hurry	more speed	more burnout
more clutter	more anxiety	more interruptions

Then progress gives us . . .

more weaponry	more terrorism	more illicit drugs
more gambling	more casinos	more pornography
more predators	more Internet viruses	more spam
more antidepressants	more fast food	more calories
more obesity	more diabetes	more heart disease
more insomnia	more entitlements	more budget deficits

It would have been difficult to anticipate that progress would strike riches with such a simple business model. Yet upon reflection, it makes perfect sense. For example, destitute people need more: more food, more clothes, more shelter. Progress supplies these needs, and everyone is benefitted. Even after modest improvement from their impoverishment, people still need more: more education, more books, more eyeglasses. Progress provides these as well. The process keeps climbing an endless ladder, progress keeps advancing, all the time improving its productivity and profits. The world marches onward and upward.

What happens when all needs and desires are met? Does progress retire? It is a nonsensical question for at least two reasons. (1) It is impossible to satiate people's needs and desires. First we want televisions, dishwashers, and CD players. Then we want RVs, cabins by the lake, and vacations to Bermuda. There is nothing specifically wrong with these desires—it is just that they never stop. Everything is not enough. *More* is always in style, and progress always has a job. (2) If we did satiate people, it would destroy the economy. This will never be allowed.

REACHED, THEN BREACHED

Many individuals, however, are now coming to a point where their limits are breached. They reach saturation and feel overloaded. They have no margin and find it a painful experience. Additional goods and services feel more like a burden than a joy. For the first time, to have more sounds less attractive and to have less sounds more attractive. These same individuals also realize they don't have enough money to play this expensive game anyway. The price tag for the good life has gone up, debt levels are mounting, and people feel stressed.

This is an awkward moment. Progress cannot have sympathy for these people's overload because its sole function is to keep the economy growing. The well-being of the economy is more important than the well-being of the individual. If people balk at buying more, this simply becomes an obstacle to overcome through advertising. Experience shows that even when overloaded and indebted, people still are easily manipulated by slick marketing. Remember, deep down, our spirits are insatiably hungry. "Give a man everything he desires," said Immanuel

Kant (1724–1804), "and yet at this very moment he will feel that everything is not everything."

The "Great Recession" of 2007–2009 was a lesson in overreach. The worst financial downturn in seventy years, it was far deeper and more refractory than anyone expected. It punished not only profligate real estate markets and financial institutions but also millions of individuals for excessive mortgages on houses too expensive for income levels. The effects ricocheted throughout the entire global economic system. Many people, both the guilty and the innocent, have been permanently scarred and will never fully recover. As horrific as this experience was, it is but a warning shot across the bow.

The Great Recession

March 2008 — Bear Stearns collapses.

September 2008 — Lehman Brothers, fourth largest investment bank, declares bankruptcy.

September 2008 — U.S. economy "fell off a cliff."

September 2008 — Treasury Secretary Paulson and Fed Chairman Bernanke propose $700 billion emergency bailout. Bernanke: "If we don't do this, we may not have an economy on Monday." Paulson, down on one knee before Speaker Pelosi, begs her support.

September 2008 — Goldman Sachs "lost a packet" for something their computers said would happen only once every 100 millennia.

September 2008 — Fannie Mae and Freddie Mac placed into conservatorship holding $5 trillion in mortgage obligations.

December 2008 — "If Citigroup goes down, it could easily take the entire world economic system with it."

December 2008 — Bernie Madoff, former Chairman of NASDAQ, jailed for operating $65 billion Ponzi scheme, largest in history.

December 2008 — S&P 500 gained or lost 5 percent of its value during a single trading day *42 times* in 2008, compared to *1 time* per year 2000–2007, and ½ *time* every year 1950–2000.

February 2009 — Davos World Economic Forum reports 40% of the world's wealth wiped out in past five quarters.

March 2009 — S&P 500 bottoms at $666, down from high of $1,565 in October 2007.

November 2009 — Unemployment hits 10.2 percent, highest in thirty years. Job losses this recession greater than the last four recessions combined.

December 2009 — Federal Budget Deficit hits $1.3 trillion; previous high $455 billion.

May 2010 — Flash Crash on May 6, Dow falls 999 points, losing $800 billion in thirty minutes, then regains $600 billion in twenty minutes. No reports on the cause for six months, and even then incomplete.

September 2010 — One-fourth of home mortgages underwater, where owners owe more on mortgage than the house's value. Average home in Merced, California, declined in value 63 percent over previous four years.

December 2010 — National Debt hits $14 trillion (2000 $5.6; 2004 $7.6; 2008 $10.7).

So, in response, what do economists and politicians want us to do? They say "save," but they mean "spend." Buy more. Open up the pocketbook. Increase retail spending. Since consumer spending and consumptive demand account for 70 percent of economic activity, we can't keep the economy healthy unless consumers actually spend money, and lots of it.

Nearly everyone who understood the meaning of this moment was frightened by it. An excruciating recession inflicting widespread unemployment and long-lasting pain caused by people, institutions, and governments spending money they did not have, must now be corrected by having these same people, institutions, and governments spend money they still don't have.

One would think at this point that we might be finding a good policy argument for contentment.

FORGOTTEN AND UNWELCOME

There is no doubt that progress has risen to impressive heights in the past twenty-five years. But is this still the "gift of God" we talked about earlier? That label only applies if progress obeys God and serves righteousness. Unfortunately, the gift has gone rogue. Loose from its moorings, progress now serves itself. It lives to maximize power, profits, and *more*, while Jesus lived to maximize love and truth. We are officially adrift from the original intent.

Of the many gifts God gave us, progress is a "power tool" kind of gift. When progress remembereth its Maker, this tool can be used freely and trusted implicitly. When detached from the Almighty, however, the trust clause is nullified. Once that happens, we must proceed with caution, knowing that progress retains great power that is no longer sanctioned. Such unsanctified power is capable of enormous damage, like gift-wrapped plutonium.

Contentment is consistent with progress as long as progress is consistent with Scripture. Once progress abandons a biblical basis and goes off in its own direction, God withdraws His Spirit. Biblical contentment drifts into the background, along with kindness, calmness, generosity, service, and rest. Then one morning we wake up to find ourselves ruptured, far afield of a truly biblical society. Contentment, so important in the Ten Commandments, in the Wisdom Literature, in the example and words of Jesus, and in the Epistles, has been banished. No longer is the presence, the provision, and the providence of God sufficient for our satisfaction. Instead, we must have *more*.

The reason for the hostility is easy to see. Were biblical contentment practiced widely, it would collapse the economy. Of course there is little worry of this happening, because in contrast to earlier eras, contentment has such a thin following today. Progress is everything. The economy is everything. Contentment? That is *so* yesterday. Contentment has been dismissed from court, and no one speaks its name.

Let me draw a comparison to the medical world. There was a time when *compassion* was a medical word and when "your ache in my heart" was an essential part of our calling. But I never hear the word compassion in a medical context today (except in faith-based organizations such as CMDA). Similarly, *contentment* in the past was a valued word in culture and literature, an important principle in theology and philosophy. Those days are gone. I hear neither the word nor the principle discussed. This is not to say that on an individual basis, people might not value it. But we do not hear it said of an important leader, "There goes a contented person." The word has been replaced by driven, aggressive, competitive, hungry, ruthless, relentless. These are the people sought after, the people who push-push-push, who get things done, who can make it happen. These are the ones pursued, promoted, and praised.

Think about it. What CEO would suggest to shareholders that contentment will help them get through a fall in stock prices? What corporate board meeting would have contentment as an agenda item? What salesperson would be encouraged to incorporate contentment into his or her work schedule? There is zero room for contentment in corporate America.

In politics, can you imagine a U.S. president in the midst of difficult economic times explaining to a television audience that contentment is a virtue? In a pure sense it might be the right thing to say, but it would sound patronizing. Approval ratings would drop ten points overnight. The opposition would loop the sound bite endlessly to show how out of touch the president was.

In education, college today is far less about reflective graduates who can discern the times and live by the highest principles than about pursuing the most lucrative careers. Medical and law students often flock to the highest paying subspecialties. Other students study business, finance, economics, and mathematics so they can learn about credit default swaps, hostile takeovers, and leveraged buyouts. Rana Foroohar, *Time* magazine's economics reporter, demonstrates this trend:

> As one mathematician turned trader friend recently put it to me, why should he work on new high-tech products at Bell Labs when he could make five times as much crafting 12-dimensional models of the stock-buying and selling behaviors of average Joes for a major global investment house, which could then turn around and make massive profits by betting against those very patterns?[5]

I do not mean to stick a thumb in the eye of all business leaders, politicians, and students—please forgive me if it sounds that way. Many are servant leaders, properly motivated to work hard on behalf of the common good. It is not wrong to have godly ambition, nor to prosper from a strong work ethic. As for intensity, it is good for a person to have passion—I have a bit of it myself. It is just unfortunate, from my perspective, that so few today choose to travel the Beatitude road.

OATMEAL AND RICE

Contrast this to the example of Hudson Taylor (1832–1905), who traveled to China 150 years ago. Yes, the terms *relentless* and *driven* applied to him, but with the opposite meaning of today. He was, for example, *relentlessly* sacrificial. He was also *driven* to seek first the kingdom of God. Missionaries serving in his China Inland Mission could neither raise funds nor mention their needs. He broke with Western traditions, insisting his workers dress in Oriental garb according to custom, including pigtails. They moved from town to town, sowing seeds of service and faith, often leaving the harvest to those who came after.

When nineteen, Taylor received a message from God: "Go for Me to China." In preparation, he left his parents' comfortable home to assist a doctor in an impoverished region. Late one night, he was called to pray for a sick woman with starving children. He tried to lift the woman before the heavenly throne, but choked on his words. He realized that in his pocket was his last silver coin, yet it was the very answer to his prayer and her desperate need. *Hypocrite*, he thought. How could he ask this woman to trust God's provision when he himself did not trust God for his own provision?

In faith, he handed the desperate woman the coin. This meant he was left with but one bowl of porridge between himself and poverty. The next day, an unsolicited, anonymous package arrived containing a gold sovereign worth ten times the silver coin. He never discovered the donor.

By such experiences, Taylor learned to trust God in every area of his life.

> I soon found that I could live upon very much less than I had previously thought possible. Butter, milk, and other such luxuries I soon ceased to use; and I found that by living mainly on oatmeal and rice, with occasional variations, a very small sum was sufficient for my needs. In this way I had more than two-thirds of my income available for other purposes. And my experience was that the less I spent on myself and the more I gave away, the fuller of happiness and blessing did my soul become.[6]

When he died in 1905 at the age of seventy-three, Taylor had founded China Inland Mission, including 260 mission stations with 825 missionary members and associates. There were an estimated 100,000 Christians in the country.

CHAPTER 5

THE SECRET OF CONTENTMENT

Increasing Our Joy and Contentment Range

I have learned to be content whatever the circumstances. I know what it is to be in need, and I know what it is to have plenty. I have learned the secret of being content in any and every situation, whether well fed or hungry, whether living in plenty or in want.

— PHILIPPIANS 4:11-12

Matt, the second of our two sons, was an aid worker in beastly hot Kurdistan in northern Iraq. It was late night in a dark, empty house with no electricity when we reached him. His only nephew had just died. Matt is not the crying type, but that night, his weeping let loose. "I am always so far away when I need to be close," he said later.

Nico Everett Swenson, eleven-month-old son of Adam and Maureen, was in a Minneapolis hospital for heart surgery. We expected an uncomplicated five-day hospitalization, but something went wrong during the procedure. The staff scrambled furiously to stabilize the hemorrhaging ventricle, barely succeeding. He remained unconscious on a ventilator through six weeks of attempts to fix his heart. Finally, a mechanical valve seemed to do the trick. Then it formed a massive clot, and Nico slid away.

People around the world had been praying, including Matt's girlfriend, Suzie. An aid worker in Afghanistan, she prayed daily against the insurgency and for Nico's recovery.

Matt was able to hop a middle-of-the-night flight to Dubai to begin the journey home. At the same time, unknown to Matt, Suzie was flying in from Kandahar. They had been apart for months, sending coded text messages between Afghanistan and Iraq. Suzie would usually fly the 300-mile Kandahar-Kabul direct route. But southern Afghanistan had grown so dangerous that, to avoid having her name on the public flight manifest, she chose the safer 1,700-mile Kandahar-Dubai-Kabul cargo-plane option. Under normal circumstances, neither would be in Dubai that day. Now both were. After a few hugs, some food, and prayer, Matt made it home for Nico's funeral, and Suzie made it safely to Kabul.

The two met doing aid work in Afghanistan for different organizations. Matt's responsibilities took him to remote airstrips across the country, repairing runways or building parking pads. When Matt first volunteered to work in Afghanistan, the organization said he would need to be buried in country if killed. Matt said okay and signed the form. Then, from a church bulletin, he tore out two lines of a song, folded it, and jammed it deep in his wallet. "Till He returns or calls me home, here in the power of Christ I stand."[1]

On one occasion, a close colleague of Matt's was walking a few blocks from their office when accosted by three men with AK-47s. Though it was mid-afternoon in a highly guarded area of Kabul, they roughed him up, pushed him into the trunk, and drove off. Preferring to avoid a hooded TV appearance, he jimmied opened the trunk latch with a tire iron and threw himself onto the street as the car sped away. Though a volunteer, he chose to remain in country for another three months.

Massoud, Matt's best Afghan friend, was a university student who guarded the house at night. One dark, cold, and snowy winter morning at 4 a.m., they were talking in Massoud's guard shack. Matt was waiting to be picked up for a stint of working on a northern airstrip. Massoud asked, "Why do you do this? Why do you stay?" Matt handed him the daily cup of Swiss Miss Hot Chocolate and said, "Just trying to help."

Later, Matt's work took him north to Mazar-e Sharif, where he relieved stress by fishing with a cane pole for carp, standing on an old Russian tank in the river bordering Uzbekistan. Suzie, meanwhile, went south to Kandahar. She had been promised help developing a huge public health project, but although the project progressed, consistent help never came. Suzie speaks Dari, is a great leader, and had an Afghan staff of forty, but still. . . . There were six other single female aid workers in this large city, a Taliban stronghold. Then Suzie's friend was captured. Beloved by the Afghan women, she was fluent in Pashto and always wore her burka. This gentle person and her driver were kidnapped on the way to work, never again seen.

One day, when Suzie was away at a meeting, insurgents came to her compound to get her. The security guards and office manager stopped them at the gate, saying she was gone. Suzie had six watchmen who rotated duties—none armed, two geriatric, one lame, one deaf and nearly blind. Given the increased threats, Suzie then moved to a "safer" area of the city and chose the cheapest option housing, inexpensive because former occupants had been decapitated there.

Another of Suzie's close friends moved to Kabul for security reasons. A few months later, she was walking to work when two men on a motorbike gunned her down. Two years later, yet another dear friend of both Matt and Suzie was massacred with nine others in the north during an eye project in remote mountain villages.

Pakistan suffered a devastating earthquake in 2005 that killed 80,000 and left 3.5 million homeless. Matt went to help. Dozens of aid agencies responded with relief programs. After false reports of a Koran desecration, the word went out, "Lockdown; demonstrations today." Matt and his roommate stayed home, sat on the roof, and watched the anti-U.S. demonstrations below.

After their wedding, Matt and Suzie went to Liberia. Their first "home" was a nice apartment, unfortunately located in an area known for witchcraft. The effects were soon apparent: repeated illnesses, dark thoughts, horrible nightmares, at times being pinned in bed and unable to move. A tiny house by the ocean was much better, but they still slept with a machete, Mace can, and deafening air horn in case intruders came through the roof. A thirteen-year civil war left the country with 75 percent unemployment. Though they loved the country and people, problems were everywhere. National staffers would get sick and be dead within days. While in the remote jungle, they occasionally met people who had never before seen a white person. Some thought Suzie was Queen of the Course, a legendary evil spirit of the river with white skin and brown hair. She quickly convinced them otherwise.

Next came Japan, where hundreds of square miles of total devastation awaited them. The power unleashing the massive 2011 earthquake under the ocean floor was 600 million times that of the Hiroshima bomb. The tsunami waves, in some places, were 128 feet high. Matt and Suzie both had supervisory roles in an organization tasked with rebuilding 500 homes and restoring hope, all while dodging the largely unknown effects of radiation from the Fukushima nuclear reactors sixty miles south.

LIGHT AND MOMENTARY TROUBLES

Millions of people have suffered far more than Matt and Suzie. Most suffering, however, is the unavoidable kind: car accidents, tornadoes, flooded basements, influenza. People do not choose to be depressed, go bankrupt, or have cancer. Seldom do people walk into the storm when they could walk around it.

Then there are the Christ followers, those who deny themselves daily, take up their cross, and follow the Messiah in word and example. The original disciples all chose this path and paid dearly. The apostle Paul, too. Never one to bypass persecution, he preferred the straight-on approach. He stormed into the storm.

Paul (Saul) was born in Tarsus, along the southern coast of modern-day Turkey. It was 275 miles directly north of Nazareth. At the same time Paul's mother was laboring to give birth, Jesus, about eight years old, was laboring in the carpenter shop with His father, Joseph.

When perhaps twelve, Paul traveled to Gamaliel's prestigious school in Jerusalem to study, later saying he was "brought up in this city."[2] During these student years, Paul was sixty-five miles directly south of Nazareth, where Jesus was also studying the Law and the Prophets.

They never met. Not until the light-and-power show near Damascus.

Paul, even though highly educated and a learned Pharisee, walked in darkness. He was a zealous persecutor of the new heretical sect. He attended the stoning of Stephen, the first martyr.[3] Still "breathing out murderous threats against the Lord's disciples," he traveled to Damascus to capture those who belonged to "the Way."[4]

But Jesus had other plans. He made the extraordinary decision to confront Paul in a way that left him few options. In speech wrapped with blinding light, Jesus knocked Paul to the ground, spoke to him directly, and left him sightless for three days. It had the desired effect. Unveiled glory works every time.

And so it was that a vicious persecutor of the church became himself persecuted for that same faith. Paul's titanic mind turned toward the light that had blinded him, transforming him into the most dominant defender of Christianity after Jesus. Why Paul? It was not for his world-class intellect. His brilliance, knowledge of theology and philosophy, writing, and articulate debating skills were useful, but God is not a respecter of persons regarding intellect. Neither was it for his credentials. Although Paul's cosmopolitan upbringing, Roman citizenship, and fluency in languages led to ease of travel, three missionary journeys, and appeal to Rome, God had the power to accomplish this through other means.

Perhaps it was Paul's utter willingness to throw himself into the fray, to suffer the worst without regard, to say "I consider my life worth nothing to me; my only aim is to finish the race and complete the task the Lord Jesus has given me—the task of testifying to the good news of God's grace."[5]

Paul's sufferings for Christ have become legendary: on display like men condemned to die in the arena, a spectacle to the whole universe, a fool, weak, dishonored, hungry, thirsty, in rags, brutally treated, homeless, cursed, persecuted, slandered, scum of the earth, refuse of the world, hard pressed on every side, perplexed, persecuted, struck down, always being given over to death, death at work in us, outwardly wasting away, in prison more frequently, flogged more severely, exposed to death again and again, five times received forty lashes minus one, three times beaten with rods, once stoned, three times shipwrecked, spent a night and a day in the open sea, constantly on the move, in danger from rivers, in danger from bandits, in danger from countrymen, in danger from Gentiles, in danger in the city, in danger in the country, in danger at sea, in danger from false brothers, gone without sleep, known hunger and thirst, gone without food, been cold and naked, stoned, dragged outside the city, stripped and beaten, severely flogged, thrown into prison, dragged from the temple, arrested, bound with two chains, taken into the barracks, flogged, in troubles, hardships, distresses, beatings, imprisonments, riots, sleepless nights, hunger, regarded as impostors, beaten, sorrowful, poor, having nothing.

And that's only seven chapters.[6] Yet, remarkably, he writes, "For our light and momentary troubles are achieving for us an eternal glory that far outweighs them all."[7] *Light and momentary?*

Paul wrote thirteen of the twenty-seven books in the New Testament and is mentioned in three-fourths of the chapters of Acts, written by his good friend Dr. Luke.

REJOICE GREATLY

One of Paul's most beloved books is his letter to the Philippians, written toward the end of his life. Even though he was in chains and under house arrest for two years in Rome, and even though he wrote of suffering for Christ and of dying, nevertheless this book is called the Epistle of Joy.

Given the setting, it seems incongruous that the words *joy* and *rejoice* are mentioned fourteen times:

I always pray with JOY
because of this I REJOICE
I will continue to REJOICE
your progress and JOY in the faith
your JOY in Christ Jesus
make my JOY complete
I am glad and REJOICE
you too should be glad and REJOICE
with great JOY
REJOICE in the Lord!
my JOY and crown
REJOICE in the Lord always
I will say it again: REJOICE!
I REJOICE greatly in the Lord

Just putting this list on the page lifts my spirits. Joy is like that. If Paul rejoiced greatly under such difficult conditions, I clearly need to increase my joy range.

LEARNING THE SECRET AND THE SPECTRUM

Paul, in his adverse circumstances and advancing age, has other surprises for us as well. Beyond commending joy, he now wants to commend the blessing of contentment. The following is the first of three remarkable passages in the Epistles on contentment: "I have learned to be content whatever the circumstances. I know what it is to be in need, and I know what it is to have plenty. I have learned the secret of being content in any and every situation, whether well fed or hungry, whether living in plenty or in want."[8]

Paul explains three important components of contentment: (1) it is to be learned, (2) it is a secret, and (3) it is to apply across the entire spectrum of life circumstances.

CONTENTMENT IS TO BE LEARNED

A man went to visit his friend near the Brooks Range in northern Alaska. It is a beautiful area teeming with wildlife but very inhospitable and sparsely populated. After a fishing trip, they were cleaning salmon together along the river. The visitor looked over at his friend, who had taken off his shirt. His back was a blanket of grey.

"Jim, your back is covered with mosquitoes."

"I know," he said as he kept working on the fish.

"Doesn't that bother you?"

"No."

"That's crazy. How can that not bother you?"

"When I came out here, I decided I had to learn a different way of living. Part of my learning was to train myself to ignore mosquitoes."

Ignoring mosquitoes is not a normal human trait. Neither is contentment. Contentment is not picked up in the natural course of living. For example, it is not acquired by simply growing older, so that at forty we are more content than at twenty. Neither is it acquired by growing richer; most commonly, the opposite is true. Nor is it attained by getting married or having children. Perhaps most surprisingly, contentment is not innate to being a Christian.

It looks, from all appearances, that discontentment is dug in for the duration, determined to stay until our last breath. The only way to dislodge this grim fortress is to learn it away. Even the great apostle Paul, by his own admission, needed to learn contentment: "I have *learned* to be content."

In *The Rare Jewel of Christian Contentment*, Jeremiah Burroughs (1599–1647) wrote,

> Contentment in every condition is a great art, a spiritual mystery. It is to be learned and to be learned as a mystery. And so [Paul] affirms, "I know both how to be abased, and I know how to abound: every where and in all things I am instructed." The word that is translated instructed is derived from the word that signifies "mystery." It is just as if he had said, "I have learned the mystery of this business." Contentment is to be learned as a great mystery.[9]

Let's look at some prescriptions that will get us started in the process of learning to be content.

Rx: 1   *Learn Through Intentionality*

Contentment is a valuable character attribute, but it is also one of the most difficult to nurture. It is not mainstream, it is not normal, it is not natural. It is, in fact, countercultural and vastly underappreciated. For those pursuing it, understand that the pursuit requires effort.

A person who wants to run a marathon discovers he or she cannot do it from a bathtub reading the paper. Because running a marathon is difficult, marathon runners are rare. Likewise, contented people are rare. A passive approach will not yield the prize. We will not get there by sitting in a lawn swing, yawning, with our eyes half-closed. If we wish to obtain the joys of a contented life, sustained intentional effort will be required.

Name it as a goal. Set it high. Be willing to pay the price. For contentment brings us not only rest of mind, peace of spirit, joy in community, and calmness in conversation, but also an unusual sense of closeness to Christ. And that is worth any price.

Rx: 2   *Learn Through Experiences*

We learn contentment through experiences but not necessarily through achievements or acquisitions. Achievements cause us to believe it is all about us, but Jesus said, "Apart from me you can do nothing."[10] Acquisitions cause us to want more acquisitions, thus feeding the obsession we are trying to conquer. In the end, life is not about awards or assets — not even in the same solar system.

Life experiences, on the other hand, are wonderful teachers if we know how to pay attention. All life experiences are spiritual experiences. The experience of mowing the lawn, changing a tire, visiting the sick, going to work, standing in line for a flu shot, or eating dinner — each is an experience where God wants our ear. Whatever our involvement, if we learn to look deeper, we will find God standing in the shadows, whispering instructions. He is always there, regardless of the occasion, asking us to trust His provision and His providence.

Paul went to the same contentment school we do. British biblical scholar and evangelist Arthur Pink (1886–1952) wrote, "The apostle did not say, 'I have received the baptism of the Spirit, and therefore contentment is mine.' Nor did he attribute this blessing to his perfect 'consecration.' Equally plain is it that it was not the outcome of natural disposition or temperament. It is something he had learned in the school of Christian experience." Paul had to practice it, grow in it, nurture it, learn it. And if Paul, an ultra-marathoner, was schooled in this manner, perhaps that is a signal to us. Minute by minute, thought by thought, experience by experience, we are changed into the image of Christ and contentment is the result.

Rx: 3   *Learn by Being in the Presence of God*

We do not learn from afar that God is a contentment kind of God. This is not something discerned through a telescope. It is learned while sitting on His lap. He is not the kind of teacher that phones it in. He is the one-to-one student-teacher ratio kind. God is very intimate, extremely personal, and has all the time in an infinity of infinities. Any deficiencies in the relationship always come from our side.

If our lives are too busy, too self-absorbed, or too full of media, and there is no room for communing with our Maker, then the experience of contentment will be an academic exercise rather than a daily reality. "Real contentment is only possible by being much in the presence of the Lord Jesus," wrote Pink. "It is only by cultivating intimacy with that One who was never discontent, that we shall be delivered from the sin of complaining. It is only by daily fellowship with Him who ever delighted in the Father's will, that we shall learn the secret of contentment."

Rx: 4   *Learn Through Patient Submission to Christ*

There are many problems in life that we should meet head-on and work to defeat. Contentment does not bind our hands or our hearts when confronting obviously correctable issues. If the kitchen drain is plugged, fix it. Hardships that obstruct our spiritual lives should be remedied as soon as possible. Difficulties that hinder our relationships should appropriately be dealt with. If we hate our jobs, we should, by all means, try to find better ones.

But what about unavoidable troubles? This is a separate category, one where contentment begs a role. Perhaps we slip on the ice and suffer a spinal fracture causing lifelong pain. Do we seethe and spit, screaming for vengeance, cursing at the vapors and yelling at the Almighty? Or do we instead say, "God has an agenda for me, and I had best get about learning it"?

The common and often understandable reactions of frustration, irritability, and bitterness do not dull the pain, they double it. But if we turn in God's direction, His gift of contentment brings a measure of peace in the midst of pain.

"But how can we learn contentment?" asks pastor and author J. R. Miller (1840–1912).

> One step toward it is patient submission to unavoidable ills and hardships. . . . There are trials which we cannot change into pleasures, burdens which we cannot lay down, crosses which we must continue to carry, thorns in the flesh which must remain with their rankling pain. When we have such trials, why should we not sweetly accept them as part of God's best way with us? Discontent never made a rough path smoother, a heavy burden lighter, a bitter cup less bitter, a dark way brighter, a sore sorrow less sore. It only makes matters worse. One who accepts with patience that which he cannot change—has learned one secret of victorious living.

Rx: 5   *Learn by Moderating Our Desires*

There has been a continuous escalation of the norm in our desires over the past decades that has scarcely been challenged. It is considered patriotic, as we have seen, to support the economy even if we don't have the money for it. Such a narrative fits easily into our natural inclination to welcome desires of all kinds.

Contentment, however, will never be learned by perpetuating the thinking that propels us in the opposite direction. At some point we will need to do three things. First, come to a complete stop. Second, think about it long enough to see the behavior. And finally, when we are ready, make a conscious turn toward the de-escalation of desires. This is a serious point, and we will not gain control of our desires until we fully understand what is at stake. It is an addiction that can be broken, but not by fluffy half-resolutions the weight of a shadow.

It is unusual for people to make large shifts in behavior, but if we are to learn contentment, we will need to challenge thinking and habits on a regular basis. Once we make the transition, we will discover a pleasant surprise: Desiring less actually increases our satisfaction.

Rx: 6   *Learn by Adjusting Our Hearts*

The spiritual heart is the repository of our affections. This makes it a target-rich environment for a study of contentment. "Set your minds on things above," Paul taught, "not on earthly things."[11] David said, "Though your riches increase, do not set your heart on them."[12] A millennium later, Jesus gave us the reasoning behind David's words, "For where your treasure is, there your heart will be also."[13]

The heart becomes easily crowded, and never more so than today. Under the reality of daily profusion, our eyes see hundreds of things to tantalize the heart. God does not need expensive tests to know the condition of our hearts, and if we love the wrong things, He gives us what we deserve: discontent.

We often feel our unhappiness comes from the misery of our surroundings, but instead it comes from our hearts. "The real cause of our discontent is not in our circumstances," said Miller. "If it were, a change of circumstances might cure it. It is in ourselves, and wherever we go we shall carry our discontent heart with us. The only cure which will affect anything—must be the curing of the fever of discontent in us."

Rx: 7   *Learn by Daily Choices*

Life is an endless series of daily choices, some mundane, others life-changing. God is most interested in those that shape our faith. Will we choose to be biblical Christians? Will we seek first the kingdom of God? Will we store up treasure in heaven rather than on earth?

In the 1930s, a missionary to the Philippines, Frank Laubach, made an interesting choice. He decided to think of God at least once every minute. I'm not sure I've ever heard of a person making such a blessedly challenging resolution. The story is also told of a South African preacher who stopped in the middle of the street, traffic speeding by. When he was later asked why, he said, "Just for a minute, I lost my connection to God." These men made the choice of intimacy with the Almighty.

Contentment is also a choice, and by making it frequently throughout the day, we train our wills to want what God wants for us. This is the process of learning to be content. Over time, the advantages of contentment become so powerful, the satisfaction in Christ so settled, that the choices in that direction become second nature.

Rx: 8   *Learn Through Patience*

Patience and contentment are good friends and travel companions. Both, however, have fallen out of favor. They simply are not consistent with modern business practices. But it is unfair to blame their unpopularity solely on the business world, for multitasking and frenzy are everywhere.

Spiritually, this presents a problem. In one verse alone, Psalm 37:7, we have three significant difficulties in just the first section of the verse: "Be still before the LORD and wait patiently for him." *Be still* and *wait* and *patiently* were all thrown out decades ago. What do we do now? "It is certain that all persons who do not learn patience are making a bad progress in the divine life," wrote John Calvin (1509–1564).

From Scotland, Douglas Taylor reflected on his diagnosis with inoperable liver cancer in May 2011.

> I have been saying for months that what I need is patience, and there is truth in this; but I have often misconstrued patience as just gritting the teeth and holding on grimly till relief comes. But now I see that, as well as patience, I need contentment. The difference I see between

the two is this: patience is passive suffering of what God sends, while contentment is active acquiescence in what he sends, being pleased and happy with it. Patience bears it, but contentment welcomes it. This is what I need more of.[14]

A hundred years earlier, Peter Ainslie, in his delightful little book *God and Me*, expressed a similar sentiment.

When things do not go as I want them, and I have used my best judgment and put into them all my energies, I must remember that my judgment is not infallible, and perhaps God is directing otherwise the affairs that concern me; but whether it be God's directing or Satan's it will eventually be for my good, for God is my friend, and He is able to overrule all things according to His will, and so I must try to practice contentment.[15]

"We must pray for the graces of contentment and patience, and a holy indifference to all the things of sense and time,"[16] wrote Matthew Henry (1662–1714) in his magnificent five-volume commentary. "It is an unreasonable thing to be weary of waiting for God."[17]

CONTENTMENT IS A SECRET

God is infinite; we are not. By definition, this means that the vast majority of God's reality must be hidden from us. We are surrounded by incomprehensible mystery. God holds the keys and unlocks only what He chooses. He reveals what He wishes according to His own timing. The rest stays unknown.

It was David who said, "The secret of the LORD is for those who fear Him,"[18] and Isaiah who wrote, "Truly you are a God who has been hiding himself."[19]

The Son of God, too, was full of secrets and often mysterious. He instructed His followers to tell no one what they had seen. He spoke in parables so that only some could understand. He told His disciples,

"The knowledge of the secrets of the kingdom of heaven has been given to you, but not to them."[20] Another time He said, "I praise you, Father, Lord of heaven and earth, because you have hidden these things from the wise and learned, and revealed them to little children."[21]

The teaching of contentment fits a similar pattern. Paul said, "I have learned the secret of being content." What does he mean? What secret? Theologian J. I. Packer said Paul chose the word *secret* intentionally. The original wording suggests he had been "initiated" into a secret teaching. He was "instructed" in a mysterious hidden truth unknown to the world but shared among the close confidants of God.

Paul did not buy his way into this secret, nor did he acquire enough merit badges to earn it. The granting of this secret is from God, and it is not available through our racking up a high enough pile of donations, good works, or frequent flyer miles. Instead, the secret comes from our faith and sanctification proven over time, and it is available even to the meekest human on earth.

The first step to gaining the secret of contentment is that we must want it. Second, we must agree to rid ourselves of the pincer claws of this world. Third, God must judge us earnest enough to make good use of it. Then we get the secret.

This secret is one of both freedom and power. When God's providence is apprehended by our soul, we realize there is no end to the spiritual riches the heavenly Father pours into our lives. We now have within us that which is above us, and our joy comes alive realizing the world no longer has access to our affections.

CONTENTMENT IS TO APPLY ACROSS THE ENTIRE SPECTRUM OF LIFE CIRCUMSTANCES

Arriving at the Dallas DFW Airport, I checked my bag and got in the security line. Two people some feet ahead drew my interest because of their foreign passports. The businesslike agent took their documents, looked them over, and asked, "Where are you from?"

"New Zealand," the man said.

After a few more questions, they passed through and chose a line for screening. When I cleared the agent, I scurried in their direction, always attracted by foreign travelers.

"I heard you say you were from New Zealand." I lifted my roller bag on the table and started taking off my shoes.

"Yes, we are," they said with smiles.

"Do you live anywhere near Christchurch where the earthquakes were?" The area had been rocked by a series of major quakes.

"Actually, we live in Christchurch."

"Oh my." My smile disappeared. "Did you have any damage?"

"Yes," the wife said. "Our house was destroyed. My place of work was destroyed. My husband's office was severely damaged."

"But we had a prepaid holiday to the U.S.," he said, "so we decided to come on the trip anyway."

"I am very sorry about your losses," I said.

Then the man said something I will never forget. "We feel strangely unencumbered."

His wife smiled.

I wish I had ten hours to spend with them. You lose everything and feel *unencumbered*? Most people, even if well-insured, would feel trammeled for years. Somehow, this interesting couple experienced contentment.

The best kind of contentment, the truest kind, is a state of feeling unencumbered. It is a state of absence of fear or anxiety about what we own or don't own. It is about freedom from comparison, regardless of what our neighbor has. It is about lack of pretense, so devastating to authenticity and so tedious to maintain. And the best kind of contentment, the very best, is divorced from circumstances.

Notice again how Paul's statement of contentment reflects this freedom from circumstances. "I have learned to be content *whatever the circumstances*. I know what it is to be in need, and I know what it is to have plenty. I have learned the secret of being content in *any and every situation*, whether *well fed or hungry*, whether *living in plenty or in want*." He describes a wide spectrum, actually, a complete spectrum, from top to bottom. Sounds impossible, doesn't it, to experience contentment across so wide a spectrum? But this gift of freedom is something God would give each of us.

It is easy for people to claim contentment when flush with success. They look at their bounty, then look at others, and declare victory. But this is a situational contentment, and it is often temporary. What happens if such people lost their jobs, health, reputations, or houses? The truth is, insecurity, not contentment, reigns in the human spirit regardless of our possession pile. It is just covered up with a layer of veneer. For most of us, one spectacularly bad day would be enough to erase decades of contentment veneer.

We are after something deeper in this book, something more abiding and more biblical. We are seeking the kind of contentment that is resilient, the kind built on rock, not on sand.

Rx: 9   *Cultivate Inner Contentment*

None of us can control the environment of our lives completely. We try, of course, and take every precaution to insulate ourselves against external shocks. Nevertheless, accidents on the road stop traffic; storms crash down trees; biopsies come back positive. The list is endless: flat tires, power outages, layoffs at work, sprained ankles, sick children.

Paul spoke directly to this, knowing that if contentment was to be of use to Christians, it must survive the difficulties of life. When he says that, whatever the circumstances, he has learned "to be content," the original wording is that he has learned "to be sufficient." It is the only time this is found in the New Testament and is suggestive of the stoic doctrine of self-sufficiency. Of course, Paul is not claiming (as the stoics did) to have this power himself, but rather that he has this power of sufficiency inside himself from Christ, through whom he could do all things.

What Paul is saying is that he has "learned" the "secret" of developing this "self-sufficiency" from Christ. Once this is in place, there is no end to the benefit. The list of Paul's trials is a daunting one, but he had within himself an internal fountain of sufficiency from God, whether he was well fed or hungry, living in plenty or in want.

We should be aware that Paul fully intends to take this experience out to the end, and to take us with him. In the extreme case, Paul asserts that adversity or prosperity no longer matter, for a quiet contentment of mind bears them both. Our peace in Christ is unbroken because we have a submission to the will of God. Whatever God allots we use with gratitude and whatever is lacking receives the same gratitude, knowing that all comes from a loving God who denies us only what we ought to be denied.

The teaching here is that houses are fine, money is fine, cars and clothes and curtains are fine—but in the end, they are only minor tools. The real narrative, the only thing that counts in the beginning and in the end, concerns our inner life. If we are disconnected from the Vine and have walked away from the Gardener, then we can do nothing. But with the connection to the Vine intact, we abide, we bear much fruit, we ask whatever we wish and it is given us, all for the Father's glory.[22]

Rx: 10 *Don't Look Back*

If only and *What if* are contentment killers. These phrases never turn back the clock, but they always turn up the pain. Contentment cannot be finalized as long as we continue to live in the past.

As a physician and a futurist, I agree with Paul when he said, "Forgetting what is behind and straining toward what is ahead, I press on toward the goal."[23] But my brain does not always behave, and since I have trillions of videotape images in my head (so do you), they often decide to play the *if only* tapes.

It is easy to become trapped in unpleasant destructive memories. It is just as easy to become trapped in memories when circumstances were much better than they are today, or to pine for the innocence of earlier dreams. But if we understood the full value of lessons learned, we would not begrudge God His methods. Heaven lies beyond the road ahead.

Rx: 11 *Place Our Relationship with Christ Above Our Relationship with Things*

When we have an abundance of possessions, we feel privileged. We enjoy lounging with our things and counting our money. When they are taken away, we fear for our lives.

The things of this world come, and then they go. Everything spawned here below behaves in exactly the same way. That is what it means to be temporal.

Christ is different. He is our forever friend. He created us. He rescued us. He is preparing a place for us. He will return to take us home. We bear His Image, and we now belong to Him.

When we understand that friendship with the world is false and foolish, we can at the same moment rejoice that friendship with God is without end. This is what Paul based his contentment on. Not on his possessions, not on his purse, not on his peers, not on his credentials, not on his circumstances, but on his relationship with the living Christ, who was his friend.

Our relationship with the world is always circumstantial and situational. Our relationship with God is unmovable and unshakable. Plus, when we love God, God actually loves us back.

Rx: 12 *Accept God's Providence over Our Preference*

Hurricane Ivan was the tenth most intense Atlantic hurricane ever recorded. After inflicting devastating damage to the Caribbean, it struck the Southeastern U.S. in September 2004.

With his south Alabama house directly in the path of the hurricane and its tornadoes, Charley and his family went to stay with relatives in the center of the state. As things began to quiet, he returned home to check on the damage. Before he left, he said, "It'll be all right. And if it's not all right, it'll still be all right." His mother's response, "That is a man profoundly at peace in the providence of God."[24]

Contentment is our glad submission wrapped in God's providence. The doctrine of providence explains that God has a plan, and that it is a perfect plan. Since He is all-powerful, it is impossible for us to thwart the plan. We either accept it or we kick against it, but regardless, the plan goes forward.

Fortunately for us, God is not only powerful but also loving, which means His plan is always a good one. Even misfortunes that don't seem "good" at the time fit into what God is accomplishing for our good and

His glory. This is part of the "secret" of contentment. We understand that even when we suffer, it is God being good to us.

This is a fixed truth, but often to us it seems a flawed theory. Our preferences frequently collide with God's providence. When that happens, discontentment boils over. We become angry at our sorry circumstances and murmur in rebellion at God's bungling. Soon we find ourselves stuck in the blind alley of misery.

Our preference is that Nico not have died at ten months and twenty-seven days. But he did. The one thing, the only thing, that healed our sorrow was knowing that the God who created him is the same God who called him back. Nico's race was run, his purpose accomplished; our hearts, though broken, were richer for having loved him. Someday we will fully understand. But for now, we are content to trust in His providence.

DENYING OURSELVES DAILY

When Matt was in high school, one evening I approached him and said something like "Matt, you need more suffering in your life." Now, don't get excited. I was just rattling his cage a bit, and he knew it. He was a good kid, had good friends, made moral decisions, and got good grades. But life was too easy, and I wanted him to have the opportunity to go deeper.

I reminded him that Jesus said if anyone wanted to become His disciple, he first had to deny himself, then take up his cross daily and follow Him.[25] "I can't think of anything you are denying yourself." Just a brief challenge offered in parental goodwill.

Now I wish he'd slow it down a bit.

In 2005, when working in Afghanistan, the governor of a northern province came to Matt's group and asked for help. "My people are so poor they're eating hay." Matt got the assignment. He took a UN flight to the capital of Tajikistan, then a fourteen-hour jeep ride to the northern Afghan border. There he crossed the bridge and walked twenty-five kilometers south into Darwaz province. According to the UN, the maternal mortality rate there was the worst in the world. They were destitute in nearly every regard. Matt helped refurbish an old Russian airstrip not used for decades and now they can call for help.

Another time he was working on a remote northern airstrip when blizzards hit. The heavy snows shut down the runway and trapped him. He later told me he'd slept for three weeks on the floor of a TB clinic.

"You what? Matt, that's a TB active zone. There are bacilli on that floor. They're after you. They're gonna kill you."

"Whatever."

If you have the nicest home in the U.S., invite Matt to stay with you for a few weeks. He will love it (so will Suzie). But the TB clinic worked okay too.

This is what the apostle Paul was speaking of, being content in any circumstance. When our contentment can range across the entire spectrum from top to bottom, this is the very definition of freedom. Most of us can hold contented with a temporary drop of ten or maybe twenty percent. But the floor of a TB clinic in destitute northern Afghanistan?

If we want to have the joy God wishes for us, we will need to expand our joy range. If we want the contentment God wishes for us, we will need to expand our contentment range. Yes, contentment is a secret. But it is the kind of secret the Father wants us to discover.

CHAPTER 6

GODLINESS WITH CONTENTMENT

Spiritual Wealth for All

But godliness with contentment is great gain. For we brought nothing into the world, and we can take nothing out of it. But if we have food and clothing, we will be content with that.

—1 Timothy 6:6-8

Everett Wilson was an upright man. Anyone who knew him would say so.

He was patient, generous, kind, and wise. I never heard an angry word. On the other hand, I heard tens of thousands of compliments. He was moral and clean living. He did not touch alcohol or tobacco. He had no vices. Well, he ate a little too much pie, if you ask me, but that was because Genevieve was such a great cook.

After they married in 1942, the following month was their first Christmas. Everett told Genevieve to fix the nicest party she could for ten people at noon on Saturday. That morning he disappeared with the car and came back with eight needy boys. Gen said, "After that party, I knew I would have a good life."

Everett was a counselor without a degree—didn't need one. People sought him out. He cared about the weak, the poor, the neglected, the immigrants. He granted dignity to all, no matter how low they regarded themselves. He confronted alcoholics and loved them back to sobriety. They'd shout at him early on; no one likes to be told they have a problem. But Everett had the strength to listen to their rants and realize it was the disease talking. He'd stick it out, and later was praised from porches and pulpits for "saving my life."

Everett Wilson was what the Bible calls an oak of righteousness.[1] I married into a good family.

When he was ten, he had an accident that changed his life. He and two friends went sledding. The hill was steep and ended in the middle of a highway. One of the three kids would stand at the bottom, look for traffic, then signal when it was safe. On this particular day, *All Clear* should have been *NO! WAIT! A monster truck is coming!* The poor kid only looked one direction, I guess.

The collision happened, the delivery truck won, and Everett entered the hospital for thirteen months.

I am not sure of the nature of the head injury, just that he was in a coma for six weeks and had a mysterious divot in the back of his head. His pastor would take the long trolley ride every day to pray at Everett's bedside, and when Dad came out of the coma there was no neurological damage. As far as he was concerned, Rev. Ekstrom saved his life. They forged a lifelong bond.

The real story was his broken femur. They slapped on a full-length cast including the knee and ankle. At one point, Everett's father, John, smelled an odor. He complained that something was wrong, but the medical team said it was okay. John finally got out his pocket knife and cut off the cast. Gangrene bubbled around the heel and ankle. The doctor wanted to amputate, but John said, "Over my dead body." Everett was always grateful he kept his leg even if it was disfigured, frozen at the knee and ankle, and many inches too short. The large lift in his shoe made for a visibly abnormal gait, but that was not so very important. He golfed, swam, canoed, belly flopped on sleds with the children, and taught them tennis and ice skating. All with a skinny, rigid, short stick of a leg. I'm not sure how, but he did.

Although his family had no money for college, Everett's patient work was so exacting that he found himself in management positions. The president of the company, who loved both his character and exemplary standards, promoted him to executive vice president. With a prominent parking space in the front of the building, he was asked to buy a fancier car. Everett wouldn't go any higher than a Chevy Impala. Asked to join the country club, he said, "I want my children swimming in the public pool." Mom bought him a special ring, an onyx stone in a gold band. "Gen, I can't wear this ring when counseling people who have so little."

I started dating Linda our senior year in high school, the same year Everett lost his job. The president of the company died and a younger group of hotshots took over. The absence of a degree and the presence of a conscience led to Dad's dismissal. If they thought he just didn't fit in to the new corporate structure, that was about right.

It took a while finding work. A "handicapped" leg and no college tarnished his interviews. But he had planned wisely and had a monumental faith in God.

A position at Caterpillar opened up that was providentially perfect. Dad thrived in their credit union for twenty years. He was an advocate for people, talked them carefully through loans, and helped people save their houses and marriages. Despite his boss saying with a smile, "Everett, we are supposed to *loan* people money," Dad would gently convince customers to fall out of love with the truck they couldn't afford.

Retirement was kind until his confusion began. Not Alzheimer's, but brain tumors called meningiomas. The battle complicated his final three years, and the last synapse ceased firing at age eighty-two. The retirement health benefits from Caterpillar were outrageously better than the hotshots would ever have provided.

Everett was the safest human being I have ever met. His looks were plain, with a bald head, large black glasses, massive jowls, and a gimpy leg. But his eyes shone with a divine kindness. Here, truly, was a man in whom there was no guile. He did not have a cynical cell in his body, nor did a sarcastic word pass his lips. His gentleness seemed inexhaustible, his smile famously winsome, his patience eternal. He could sit flat on the floor, bum leg angled off to the side, and build Lego towers or play Chutes and Ladders with the kids for hours. The children always gave up before he did.

He was Sunday school superintendant for twenty-five years, served on the Salvation Army board, helped an inner-city church start a new school, and gave generously to an orphanage for handicapped children. During the aftermath of the Vietnam War, Laotians who fought for our side fled for their lives and eventually ended up in the U.S. Every family had tragic stories. Dad and Mom helped them find apartments, clothes, furniture, and entry-level jobs. It didn't stop there. They became one big family, and seventy-five would arrive at the Wilsons' for a picnic. Mom and Dad knew them by name.

Late at night, Dad received a call from the police station; one of his sponsored boys was in trouble. He went straightway to intercede, assuring the police that the teenager could be released to him, that he would talk it through with the lad and his father, and that the officers would not see this young man again. In return, the record was expunged. When Dad died, there were twelve young Laotian men in black suits as pallbearers, some driving thousands of miles. We all cried.

Linda wrote, "I think my dad would always have been a good guy regardless. But with the accident and the short, stiff leg, big shoe, and moving through life at a slower pace, Dad became an oak of righteousness. The world was less kind the day he died, yet also kinder through his example and the people he blessed."

GODLINESS + CONTENTMENT = GREAT GAIN

We come now to Paul's second important teaching on contentment found in 1 Timothy 6:6-12 and anchored by the verse: "But godliness with contentment is great gain."

It is fine to discuss this verse with words but far more effective to see it lived out in front of us. Everett embodied godliness with contentment, and it was great gain. There is no earthly reason he should have had the far-reaching impact he did. He was a humble man with no birth advantages, no pedigree, no wealth, no higher education, no political connections, and no grandiose visions of self-importance. Yet I can say with confidence that if the world were populated by seven billion Everetts, our problems would disappear.

Why would problems disappear? Because godliness with contentment is great gain.

Can you imagine a world with no more harshness, no more divisions, no more indifference toward suffering? Where people were advocates for one another, where service was paramount and pride was forbidden? Where every morning and every meal began with prayer and every evening ended with thanksgiving? There would be no more privation because Everett believed in hard work, and he also believed in sharing generously. He believed in cooperation over competition and was the type who would help his neighbor even if it hurt his own situation.

He affirmed and encouraged everyone he met. He thanked you repeatedly even for small things. His patience was world-class. Can you imagine such a world?

How is this possible? Because godliness with contentment is great gain.

It is important for us to understand that even if it is only rarely achieved, *it is possible for us to live godly, contented lives.* Even when the Bible seems hopelessly impractical, there are those among us who actually succeed in honoring God above all else. And God, in turn, keeps His promise: "Those who honor me I will honor."[2]

There is another part to this story that has so far been underrepresented. When Everett was perhaps seventy, we went to a men's Bible study one morning at his church. I don't remember the topic being discussed, but I do remember Dad saying to the circled group, "I don't understand why God allowed me to have this accident." He was not complaining, just reflecting. Still, I was stunned. First, I had never heard him talk about his leg in those terms. And second, because I *did know* why God allowed it.

"Dad, I know why. He was building Everett Wilson. He was building your character, your patience. Your gentleness."

When you thought of Everett, you also thought, to some degree, of his leg. But no one got hung up on it. No one pitied him for it — that was unnecessary. The bum leg was just there, an integral part of a lovely man, so it, too, was lovely in a way. People loved and respected him *more* for his leg, not less. I never felt sorry for him. And if I could go back and change history at the bottom of that hill, how dare I think I could improve on God's good work, that I could come up with a better Everett.

I shudder to think what impudent fools we sometimes are, that we can challenge the providence of God and thus destroy masterpieces.

Godliness is an attitude whereby what we want is to please God. *Contentment* is accepting from God the circumstances in which He has placed us, because we know that His presence, provision, and providence are far greater than Harvard, the country club, and a normal leg.

FOOD AND CLOTHING

An elderly grandmother was visiting her granddaughter's home for the first time. As the granddaughter worked diligently in the kitchen, the grandmother became philosophical. "Which thing in the kitchen do you like the most? You know, the thing you couldn't do without."

The young granddaughter stopped her work and thought for a minute. "I'm not sure, Grandma. I guess the microwave," she said. "What about you?"

"Oh, for me it's easy. I would pick running water."

How soon we lose awareness of our most basic needs, and how soon that lost awareness results in lapsed gratitude. God obviously allows us much more than our basic needs, for He is a generous Father. But it pleases Him when we remember to give thanks for running water. And maybe, while we are at it, we should throw in garbage pick-up and flush toilets, too.

Contentment is much easier when we remember "from his fullness we have all received, grace upon grace."[3] A cofounder of the computer-chip maker Intel said that, according to their research, people's attention starts to wander after one-half of a second. With such relentless distractibility, how can we recall God's long record of being kind to us?

If we could choose just two things in life, two categories of needs that we would miss more than all others, what would they be? In essence, we are allowing Grandma to question us: "Which two things in life do you like the most? You know, the two things you just couldn't do without."

The first choice would be unanimous. Food, including water. No debate.

What about the second choice? I suppose it would be clothing. (For those in my age range, it would definitely be clothing.)

Some people in central Wisconsin might consider shelter as the second choice, understandable given our occasional minus-fifty wind chills. However, if we choose shelter over clothes, that means we would have the much-needed roof but not the much-needed raiment, thereby losing not only our clothes but our friends as well.

"For we brought nothing into the world, and we can take nothing out of it," Paul said in this passage. "But if we have food and clothing, we will be content with that."[4]

Paul is not precluding all other possessions. God is not that strict, and the Bible is not that impractical. We are surrounded by innumerable blessings that have been created for us to use and enjoy. But can't we at least be grateful for food and clothing? Must we always take them for granted when in fact they are so fundamentally vital? Taking a giant step further, it is godliness to say, "Yes, Father, if it comes to that—food and clothing only—I pledge you my contentment."

It is interesting to notice that Paul emphasized the same two items Jesus spoke of in the Sermon on the Mount. "Therefore I tell you, do not worry about your life, what you will eat or drink; or about your body, what you will wear. Is not life more than food, and the body more than clothes?"[5] He goes on to show how the Father feeds the birds of the air and clothes the lilies of the field in splendor. "So do not worry, saying, 'What shall we eat?' or 'What shall we drink?' or 'What shall we wear?' For the pagans run after all these things, and your heavenly Father knows that you need them."[6] Strong words in the contentment direction. Why, I wonder, can I read this a thousand times without flinching?

If Jesus and Paul, the two towering giants in the New Testament, both mention food and clothing, it begs our attention.

Food

It is good to thank God for every morsel placed before us, remembering we came into the world without food and, even now, have precious little to do with its arrival on our plates. "Oh," you protest, "I work hard for my food." No doubt, and I applaud you for it. But have we so soon forgotten grace? The soil, seed, germination, water, and sun are purely gifts.

Take our sun, for example. Like all stars, it is a nonstop thermo-nuclear explosion producing light in the form of photons. We receive one-billionth of the photons, just the right amount. If the sun suddenly stopped shining, we would have eight and a half minutes before the earth plunged into complete darkness. Although we would see the stars, we would never again see the moon. The outside temperatures would plummet. Plants would die, followed by animals. Water would freeze, and fish would perish.

Do you still think food is not grace? Do we "work hard" to keep the sun shining?

An EMP bomb (electromagnetic pulse bomb) would accomplish the same result. A nuclear explosion goes off high in the atmosphere and, from horizon to horizon, everything that requires electronics would cease to function. No cars, lights, phones, computers, communication, banks, furnaces, air conditioners, refrigeration, nothing. No electricity coming into the house. No machine in the kitchen or garage would work. The average city has about seven days of food. With no functioning trucks, trains, or planes—how would we get more food? How would we get money? How would we get to work, especially when there is no longer any work? Anarchy would follow. Life would become nasty.

Do you still think food is not grace? After such an event, victims would never again take food for granted.

In the 1980s, I remember the story of a woman from New York City hosting a Russian visitor. They toured the Big Apple and saw the sights. The Russian visitor was unimpressed. "We have tall buildings in Moscow too . . . We have sports stadiums too." On it went: Russia has subways, parks, plays, concerts, the ballet. Finally, exhausted from touring, they headed home. The host quickly ran into a supermarket to pick up a few items. The Russian lady entered the store, froze in her tracks, and then started sobbing. Not even in her wildest dreams had she imagined thousands of different food items in one place.

Clothing

I remember a picture of a man from Ethiopia. Everything in his "statistically typical household" was placed in front of his 320-square-foot manure-plastered home for the photo. There were a smattering of cooking and serving utensils, baskets, a bed, a cow hide, various farm animals, a wife and five children, and a radio with a dead battery. The man was interviewed about his life. When added up, he worked eighty hours a week, his wife more. Solace in the midst of difficult conditions came from his Ethiopian Orthodox Christian faith. Finally, there was a question about his dreams. "What do you wish for the future?" It would be nice, he said, to have more farm animals and implements, better seed for planting, education for his children, and a second set of clothes. But most of all, world peace.

A second set of clothes?

The man was dressed in Ethiopian garb that seemed appropriate for his central highlands farm. But, apparently, this was his only set of clothes. We often obsess not only about clothes but about fashion itself.

Fashion models make obscene sums parading around with pretty faces and anorectic bodies displaying outfits impossible to imagine on anyone I know. At least for me, my new farmer friend is a fashion model of a different sort. His is the picture I will tear out and tape to the wall of my mind. A person content in his meagerness who thinks that additional clothes would be nice but, most of all, that his children might have schooling and the world might have peace.

Does God expect us to be content with a single pair of jeans? One loaf of bread? I don't think so. Will I empty my closet tomorrow? Doubt it. This passage is not suggesting we become John-the-Baptist-like ascetics, nor Spartans who live on an olive per day. We do not have to dress in rags to please God.

The Almighty does not despise clothes, nor sofas, ladders, or books. (Actually, He *loves* books.) He does not spit in the eye of homeowners. Jesus Himself worked on houses during His carpentry days. But everything is spiritual before it is material, and the Creator of all things expects us to get it right.

It is my strong suspicion that almost everything the Bible says, I choose to underestimate.

God will never lower His standards to accommodate the excesses of our culture. And right now, the descriptor *excess* is a diagnostic bulls-eye.

TEMPTATION, TRAP, RUIN, DESTRUCTION

Before Matt and Suzie went to Japan last year, we had a brief discussion regarding salaries and money in general. In an almost offhanded manner, I told Matt that I had not worked for money a day in my life. It was a casual comment and not thoroughly considered.

Later, I mentioned it to Linda, and we had an interesting discussion. Our conclusion: the statement is not far off. To mention this is not to claim some special kind of piety or sainthood. It is just that the Bible speaks relentlessly about the devastation awaiting people who wander too far over the line about money. I respect that line more than you can imagine.

Read slowly the following verses from Paul and linger on each word of warning.

> Those who want to get rich fall into **temptation** and a **trap** and into many **foolish** and **harmful** desires that **plunge** people into **ruin** and **destruction**. For the love of money is a root of all kinds of **evil**. Some people, eager for money, have **wandered from the faith** and **pierced** themselves with many **griefs**.[7]

Although the Bible is full of such passages, this is one of the most dire. We should not underestimate what Paul is telling us. If we fail regarding the love of money, we risk being pierced and plunged into ruin, destruction, evil, and grief.

I have such a respect for the dangers of money, how recklessly we compromise, and how devastating our fall, that I have always preferred to steer clear. I have never desired, for a second, to be rich. Linda, too, has neither wanted nor needed an elevated lifestyle. We will continue our path.

My approach is perhaps a bit foolish given the age in which we live. The world is brutally unforgiving to those whose bills have risen faster than their ability to pay. This development concerns me greatly. We are on a trajectory of escalating expenses forcing us to think more and more about money to the exclusion of much higher priorities.

FLEE TO FAITH

When Paul warns about the dangers of loving money, he does not simply tell us to *avoid* such dangers but to *flee* them. What does *flee* mean? If we see a monster F-5 tornado coming over the hill, we don't meander to the basement, we don't take the long way around, we stumble and scream down the stairs until safe. There is a serious intentionality inherent in the word *flee*. It is a word used only in serious occasions.

This might sound ominous except for the hopeful teaching that comes next. "But you, man of God, flee from all this, and pursue righteousness, godliness, faith, love, endurance and gentleness. Fight the good fight of the faith."[8] Speaking for myself, this does not remove my urgency, but it certainly removes my fear. What could be better than fleeing to righteousness, godliness, faith, love, endurance, and gentleness?

Here are some prescriptions that might help us discover godliness with contentment in our own lives.

Rx: 1 *Regard Godliness with Contentment as a Form of Wealth*

There are many different kinds of wealth. It goes without saying that in today's world, *to be rich* is thought of in monetary terms, measured by the things that can be converted into money—gold, silver, stocks, bonds, land, houses. While these can be blessings from the hand of God, all agree they are temporary. They have a beginning and an end.

Would it not be much better to have a portion of "the boundless riches of Christ," the kind that are deep and wide and uncountable and never end?[9] These riches were given us by Jesus who, "though he was rich, yet for your sake he became poor, so that you through his poverty might become rich."[10] What kind of riches? Rich in faith, with the promise of a wonderful inheritance offered especially to the humble: "Has not God chosen those who are poor in the eyes of the world to be rich in faith and to inherit the kingdom he promised those who love him?"[11] In living for Christ, we are rich in spiritual treasures both here and on the other side: "But lay up for yourselves treasures in heaven. . . . For where you treasure is, there will your heart be also."[12]

God is rich in all things good, and He shares these continuously with us. Not only does He supply our material needs, but even more, He gives us riches in the things that matter most, such as faith, love, mercy, grace, goodwill, kindness. The degree to which we value these gifts versus the monetary gifts is a measure of our progress along the "godliness with contentment" scale.

Toward the end of this section we have been discussing, Paul wrote,

Command those who are rich in this present world not to be arrogant nor to put their hope in wealth, which is so uncertain, but to put their hope in God, who richly provides us with everything for our enjoyment. Command them to do good, to be rich in good deeds, and to be generous and willing to share. In this way they will lay up treasure for themselves as a firm foundation for the coming age, so that they may take hold of the life that is truly life.[13]

Be assured, the wealth of this world will end. One day, it will be completely extinguished, never again to rise and distract us. The wealth found in godliness, however, will never end. Not only that, but while monetary riches are stratified in our society, the wealth found in godliness with contentment is equally available to all.

Rx: 2 *Refuse Piercing — and Plunging, Too*

Paul uses such dramatic language in this section that even a glance induces perspiration and nightmares. Was he just in the middle of a literary flourish, or did he actually mean to be so gruesome? *Temptation, trap, foolish, harmful, plunge, ruin, destruction, evil, wander from faith, pierced, griefs* — that's quite a string. No reasonable person could skim this without registering at least a 5.8 quake somewhere in their cranium. Again, God does allow wealth and clearly blesses people in that direction, but the parameters are narrowly drawn and, unless we don't mind being pierced and plunged, we should try to remain within specifications.

Money has a particular knack for domination. It takes control of people large and small, rewrites their brains, and keeps them rolling the dice, throwing caution to the wind. Bishop Horne (1730–1792), university president and preacher, wrote, "Of all things here below, wealth is that on which poor deluded man is chiefly tempted, even to the loss of life, to place his confidence; and when riches increase, it proves a hard task for the human heart to keep its affections sufficiently detached from them."

Poverty carries its own particular set of problems, painful enough. But the opposite problem, a foolhardy lusting after riches, carries a spectacular penalty for those overreaching risk-takers with a gambler's mentality. The morning after, as headlines scream the juicy news, they are disgraced, despised, accused, fired, sued, bankrupt, divorced, indicted, and imprisoned — just as Paul predicted.

Rx: 3   *Despise Not a Humble Estate*

One of the clearest teachings in Scripture is that God aligns Himself with the humble. He explicitly exalts humility. To despise what God exalts is a terrible career move.

> Clothe yourselves with humility toward one another, because, "God opposes the proud but shows favor to the humble." . . . Humble yourselves before the Lord, and he will lift you up. . . . For those who exalt themselves will be humbled, and those who humble themselves will be exalted. . . . Be completely humble and gentle. . . . Do nothing out of selfish ambition or vain conceit. Rather, in humility value others above yourselves.[14]

This is the example of Christ, who made Himself nothing, became a servant, took on human likeness, humbled Himself, and was obedient to death. How was this rewarded? "Therefore God exalted him to the highest place."[15]

If humility is a state that pleases God, it is also a state that is easier to sustain and more conducive to a contented life. When we have nothing to prove, no one to keep up with, are content with simple righteousness in daily affairs, and maximize love instead of possessions, the cost is less, the pressure is less, and we spend less time looking over our shoulder. "Contentment does not dwell so often in palaces as in the homes of the humble," wrote J. R. Miller.

Rx: 4   *Remember the Double Narrative*

We live in a reality tunnel. God does not. Because of our limited perspective, our judgments are flawed. For example, ringing throughout the chambers of our tunnel is the message that money is everything. It is quite natural, then, that people should fall in love with it.

God is highly offended by such nonsense. He knows that money is only green paper, gold is but shiny rocks, and silver is merely the element one proton up from palladium. These are tools of exchange that are assigned value because of what they can buy.

Simply as a thought experiment, let's return to the EMP bomb. If such a nuclear explosion went off in the upper atmosphere today, our reality would change. So would the status of money. One week from now we might try to buy food with dollars, gold, and silver, but no one would accept our offer. The food supply in town would be nearly depleted with no guarantee of new deliveries. Banks and ATMs would also be nonfunctioning. Would it still be true that "money is everything"? Just that quickly, *money is everything* would be replaced by *food is everything*.

In January 2009, Zimbabwe's national bank introduced a $50 billion note. It bought two loaves of bread. A few months later, they introduced a $100 trillion note. It could not even buy a bus ticket.

In the Weimar Republic following WWI, the German mark was so rapidly inflating that the government required 1,783 printing presses churning twenty-four hours a day to print money. People took shopping carts filled with trillions of marks into grocery stores to buy a loaf of bread. By November 1923, it required $4.2 trillion marks to equal one U.S. dollar.

According to the 2009 Davos World Economic Forum, 40 percent of the world's wealth was destroyed in the previous five quarters.

For four thousand years, God has been trying to show us the two realities, always beckoning us to understand that there is a much larger truth outside our tunnel experience. Part of this message is that money, gold, and silver are tools, not truth. We have permission to use them as tools but never permission to fall in love with them.

Spiritual riches, on the other hand, are indeed truth. They are not tools but instead the incomprehensible and unsearchable riches of God made available to us through Christ. As Peter explained, we have been given an inheritance that is incorruptible, that can never perish, spoil, or fade, kept in heaven for us. We have a faith of greater worth than gold. We know that it was not with perishable things such as silver or gold that we were redeemed from the empty way of life handed down to us from our forefathers, but with the precious blood of Christ.[16]

Things are not as they seem, God is always right, and someday soon we will understand it with perfect clarity. In the meantime, sure, let's go ahead and be practical and use the financial tools God has given us. Let's also be careful never to cross the line and start loving the garden rake rather than the Gardener who gave it to us.

ENDING WELL

I often marveled at how Everett attracted other people. When they saw him, their faces would light up and they would march over for one of those bear hugs that banished the world's problems. If you were not the huggable type, it would be that smile and kindly chuckle and the strong handshake. He always held on and looked you in the eye until you understood he meant it.

Is that what drew people to him? If so, it was coupled with his kindness and gentleness, and the pull of love, and because everything near him seemed safe.

Do you suppose godliness with contentment had anything to do with it? Do you suppose godliness with contentment would be an attractive feature for people to notice in us? I like to think so.

Meningiomas are normally benign tumors in the brain. Not Everett's. The first one, the tennis ball, was removed from the left frontal area. Then came seven more. He had many procedures, all merely slowing the inevitable. As the tumors occupied more and more of his cranium, a few behaviors emerged that were different. Then a few uncharacteristic words. Frustration was increasing because he couldn't do much and couldn't remember anything. The oak of righteousness was still with us, but his limbs were drooping and his leaves turning brown. Winter was in the air.

After his final surgery, we visited in the hospital. The procedure was near the speech and motor centers. His world was closing in, his confusion increasing. We asked him where he was, but he didn't know. Nor the year, nor the state, nor his name, nor our names.

Then Genevieve walked in. Everett's head turned toward the door. His face brightened. This woman he knew. His eyes twinkled, the smile returned. He slowly, pitifully inched his wounded body over in bed, bandaged head, stick leg, and all. Then he patted the sheets next to him, inviting her to climb in.

His was a life well lived. Because godliness with contentment is great gain.

CHAPTER 7

BE CONTENT . . . BECAUSE GOD

Commended and Commanded

Keep your lives free from the love of money and be content with what you have, because God has said, "Never will I leave you; never will I forsake you."

— Hebrews 13:5

Thomas Vincent was educated in London during the seventeenth century and remained there to preach. Exceptionally devout, he was said to have memorized the New Testament and Psalms. In 1662, a new law was passed against those who refused loyalty, or conformity, to the Church of England, such as Puritans, Presbyterians, Baptists, and Quakers. It resulted in the expulsion of more than two thousand pastors. Vincent was among those removed (ejected), which meant he could never hold a license for church work or a position in the government. He continued his ministry, nevertheless, preaching privately and working with youth at a nonconformist academy.

All this was but preparation for the ministry God set before him in 1665. The flea-spread bubonic plague, by now known and feared, made its terrifying return to England. As the black death stretched its fingers into the houses and alleys of London, hordes fled the city of half a million, including many doctors and most of the ministers. Vincent remained, despite the earnest advice of friends and other pastors. He gladly accepted their prayers but expressed hope "that none would endeavour to weaken his hands in this work."[1]

His subsequent book, *God's Terrible Voice in the City*, is a blow-by-blow account of the epidemic and makes for fascinating but grim reading. The first week's posting revealed nine deaths. Anxiety grew, then quickly abated when the next week's tally was only three.

The respite was short, however, as the deaths spiraled upward to fourteen, then seventeen, then forty-three. "Now secure sinners begin to be startled, and those who would have slept quietly still in their nests, are unwillingly awakened. A great consternation seizeth upon most persons. . . . Now those who did not believe an unseen God, are afraid of unseen arrows."

The weekly numbers continued their gruesome climb: 112, 168, 470. "Now the highways are thronged with passengers and goods, and London doth empty itself into the country."

The next month confirmed the worst: 725, 1039, 1843, 2010. "Now the plague compasseth the walls of the city like a flood, and poureth in upon it."

Then 2817, 3880, 4237, 6102. "Now people fall as thick as leaves from the trees in autumn when they are shaken by a mighty wind. . . . Now the nights are too short to bury the dead."

Then 6988, 6544, 7165. "Now the grave doth open its mouth without measure."

In the first year alone, 62,000 died. Before the disease decided to move on, 100,000 perished, 20 percent of the city's population.[2]

Vincent felt compelled to stay. Pastors, he reasoned, had an even greater burden to remain than doctors, "as the need of souls were greater than the need of bodies, the sickness of the one being more universal and dangerous than the sickness of the other, and the saving or losing of the soul being so many degrees beyond the preservation or death of the body, so the obligation upon ministers was stronger and the motive to preach greater."[3]

Though given no special sign from God regarding his protection, he traveled fearlessly from street to street, house to house, ministering to the sick and dying. Seven of the inhabitants at the house in which he lived succumbed, yet he labored on with never a sign of illness. With so many empty pulpits, he preached to large crowds every Sabbath with strong response.

As if the black plague were not enough, immediately on its heels was the 1666 Great Fire of London. Starting early Sunday morning in a bakery on Pudding Lane, by Thursday the inferno had destroyed over 80 percent of the buildings in central London, including eighty-seven parish churches, Saint Paul's Cathedral, and most of the city offices. Vincent wrote,

> Many thousands who on Saturday had houses convenient in the city, both for themselves, and to entertain others, now have not where to lay their head; and the fields are the only receptacle which they can find for themselves and their goods; most of the late inhabitants of London lie all night in the open air, with no other canopy over them but that of the heavens.[4]

What is a person to do under such overwhelming circumstances? Vincent answers that in another book, *The True Christian's Love to the Unseen Christ*.

> If you have but little love to Christ, you will be apt to faint in the day of adversity, to shrink when you are called to take up His cross and suffer for His sake. Lesser sufferings will decompose you, greater sufferings will frighten you and amaze you, and you will be in danger of turning into fearful apostates in time of great trials. There is need of great love to Christ, as well as great faith, to carry you through sufferings with courage that you may persevere unto the end.[5]

Thomas Vincent is remembered for his love to all people and his faithful service to the kingdom. Despite opposition from entrenched religious institutions, despite laws that inflicted fines and imprisonment, despite the hideous plague that depopulated the city and an equally destructive fire that claimed a large percentage of the buildings, Vincent simply refused to leave.

I WILL NEVER LEAVE YOU

Why would Vincent stubbornly remain against all reason and odds? Because love is like that. Why is love like that? Because God is like that.

> Never will I leave you; never will I forsake you.

Vincent was steadfast in not forsaking the people of London regardless of the cost to him, because God Himself had shown this same behavior. God never forsakes His people. He demonstrated it in Gethsemane and on Golgotha. Jesus wanted to pull back, but He stuck it out. Even when He sweat great drops like blood, even when they slapped a circle of needles into His head, even when they stripped Him naked and flogged Him with leather thongs embedded with iron balls, even when they hammered spikes through His bones, even—in the ghastliest of all moments—when He became sin for me, even when the Father turned His face away, even when the Messiah cried out, "My God, my God, why have you forsaken me?" Do you think, after all He has gone through, He would abandon us now?

This is the greatest kind of security, to know that God is our friend and nothing can separate us from Him. To those who belong to His family, not even London's pestilence and fire, not even the Four Horsemen of the Apocalypse,[6] not death nor life nor angels nor demons nor the present nor the future nor powers nor height nor depth—nothing can separate us from God's love.[7] Why? Because just as Vincent refused to leave London in its darkest hours, God refuses to leave us. He never forsakes His people. Jesus will never give up His grasp on my soul.

God is emphatic in making this assertion, using the word "never." Biblical scholar Arthur Pink wrote,

> It is almost impossible to reproduce in English the emphasis of the original, in which no less than five negatives are used to increase the strength of the negation, according to the Greek idiom. Perhaps the nearest approximation is to render it, "I will never, no, never leave thee, nor ever forsake thee." At no time, under any circumstances conceivable or inconceivable, for any possible cause, will God utterly and finally forsake one of His own. The continued presence of God with us ensures the continued supply of every need.

We — humans, governments, institutions, corporations, the world — are not that way. Everything here below has a tendency to leave. Money, houses, property, cars, jobs, health, friends, family — all have a tendency to grow wings and take flight. While economic downturns expose the problem more starkly, even in good times, our strength, attractiveness, hair, and vision have a way of disappearing. But God says, "I will never, ever, under any circumstances, leave or forsake you."

I had just finished speaking to a group of corporate petroleum researchers when another presenter approached me with a smile. In a previous life he had been a theologian-clergyman, but after a personal crisis, he switched careers. Being brilliant and multiply-gifted, he began writing and giving presentations on trends in technology. Reflecting on my margin material, he launched into his story. Six years earlier, he was lying in a hotel room in Salt Lake City at 3 a.m. His family had just left him, and he was suicidally depressed. In a last-ditch effort to hold on, he searched the phone book for "dial-a-prayer." As bizarre as it sounds, this clergyman dialed the number. An answering machine responded, "The number you have dialed has been disconnected." In the middle of his despair, the man decided he could either laugh or commit suicide.

"As you can guess," he said with a smile, "I laughed."

God will never treat us this way. Even if our spouse and children defriend us and dial-a-prayer is disconnected, God is still there. He will never, no, never leave us, nor ever forsake us.

KEEP YOUR LIVES FREE FROM THE LOVE OF MONEY

Hebrews 13:5 is a compact verse that carries a big punch in three short sections. The first concerns our covetous love of money; the second concerns our contentment; the third, as we have seen, concerns God's unshakable faithfulness. This last phrase anchors the first two.

(1) Keep your lives free from the love of money
and
(2) be content with what you have,
because
(3) God has said, "Never will I leave you; never will I forsake you."

The first phrase, *Keep your lives free from the love of money*, has been translated in two ways. Earlier translations read, in effect: *let your conversation, or your manner of life, be without **covetousness**.*[8] Later translations read, in effect: *Make sure your character and your life are free from the love of **money**.*

The earlier translations speak of covetousness, while the later translations speak of money. Far from being a conflict, these are merely two expressions of the same issue. Biblical scholar William Plumer (1802–1880) explained,

> There are two words in the Greek Testament which may be rendered covetousness. The one literally signifies the love of money; the other a desire of more. . . . These two senses are co-existent, for no man desires more of that which he does not love; and as he that loves silver [money] cannot be satisfied with the silver which he already possesses, he will of course desire more.

You can perhaps see that coveting, a term seldom used today, is an umbrella that covers a variety of discontentment, whether lusting after money or anything else. In many ways, an Old Testament Jewish understanding of the principle of contentment would be anchored directly in the important tenth commandment: *Thou shalt not covet*. Jesus often referred to this commandment, adding His own warning against coveting. It is no surprise, then, that Hebrews, a book directed to Jews rather than Gentiles, would also speak in these same terms.

It is perhaps readily apparent that contentment is opposed to covetousness in all its many forms. How can we tell if we are covetous? Thomas Watson, author of *The Art of Divine Contentment* in the seventeenth century, also wrote a treatise on the Ten Commandments. Here he gives "six particulars" of "What it is to covet." They hold up well today.

- When our thoughts are wholly taken up with the world
- When we take more pains for getting earth than for getting heaven
- When all our discourse is about the world
- When we so set our hearts upon worldly things, that for the love of them, we will part with heaven
- When we overload ourselves with worldly business
- When our hearts are so set upon the world, that, to get it, we will use unlawful means

There are dozens of such particulars in today's world, but from my observations, only two types of coveting are still regarded wrong in our society: coveting our neighbor's wife (spouse) and coveting something enough to steal. All other definitions go largely unchallenged.

Much modern advertising is aimed to induce peer coveting. If fifteen-year-olds see their friends with designer Jordan shoes, the hottest fashion, or the latest technology, it is fully expected this will begin a cascade of coveting—not just admiring the item, but excessively desiring it to the point of fixation. In extreme instances, teens have killed peers for their shoes, jackets, or phones.

It is no small thing to have this trend normalized both in advertising and in social settings, something we seem to have accomplished without resistance even among those who have no money. Youth and adults so wish for in-vogue acceptance that previous barriers have vaporized. Additionally, it is now hardwired into the DNA of our economy, built into the system to such an extent that if such covetous passions were to stop, it would put a sizable portion of our consumptive economy at risk.

Coveting is an internal occurrence, a desire. Although the object is usually external, the coveting itself occurs somewhere inside our skin. This makes it different from other commandments, such as don't lie, don't kill, don't make idols. Those are external and easy to distinguish. But I can covet your things so quietly that only God sees it happening.

We all have a place within us that bubbles with desire. This, in itself, is not bad. Desire is a capacity given by God for beneficial and enjoyable reasons. It is good to desire God, our spouse, friendship, food, or a good job. There is a line, however, when this cauldron of desire bubbles into excess. When *desire* becomes *inordinate desire*, it is covetousness, it is sin, and it is dysfunction. Problems always result.

Unfortunately, the boundaries between the good kind of desiring and the bad kind have become so fuzzy they are almost of no use. The lack of a clear line constitutes a major society-wide problem. Our covetousness conscience no longer works.

Even the stoical apostle Paul, that giant of self-denial, spoke of the difficulty: "I would not have known what sin was had it not been for the law. For I would not have known what coveting really was if the law had not said, 'You shall not covet.' But sin, seizing the opportunity afforded by the commandment, produced in me every kind of coveting."[9] If Paul had such internal difficulty with the tenth commandment, what does that mean for the rest of us if that part of our conscience is nonfunctioning?

The profusion of our age—*more and more of everything at exponential rates*—feeds this cauldron of discontent like never before. The object of our affection is not singular but plural and continuously growing.

Because it is internal, we can hide this issue from others and even from ourselves. We don't talk about it today and perhaps don't realize it is happening. But we certainly think it, we do it, and we enjoy it. There is nothing more wrongly pleasurable — and deadly — than participating with abandon in a sin we enjoy once modernity has removed the moral prohibition.

There are varying aspects of covetousness, such as envy, avarice, jealousy, gluttony, lust, yearning, passion, craving, longing, indulgence. Even a quick glance reveals that some of these are mild, while others are more severe. Envy is the worst.

Envy is notoriously listed among the traditional seven deadly sins.[10] It is malignant and spreads like cancer. In most situations, envy is regarded as irredeemable, and as such, is one of the biggest sources of unhappiness.

The reason for envy's dastardly reputation is that it goes beyond wishing we had another's possessions or advantages. It takes the additional step of resentment, wishing the other person were injured, disgraced, or bereft so I could then feel better. Aristotle said it is "pain at the good fortune of others." Kant said envy "is a propensity to view the well-being of others with distress. . . . It aims, at least in terms of one's wishes, at destroying others' good fortune." Dante defined it as "a desire to deprive other men of theirs." Aquinas said, "envy is sorrow for another's good."

It is this desire to injure others that God so disdains. He will judge their excesses, if any, and in the meantime, I stand before Him alone with my own faults. Envy constitutes a compounding of these faults — first, the lack of contentment on my part, and second, the wish for affliction upon another.

We have seen the pain and penalty of covetousness, whether a love for money or an inordinate desire for anything else. How might we escape such a pervasive wind, blowing so furiously throughout our consumerist society? "What means should we use to keep us from coveting that which is our neighbor's?" wrote Watson. "The best remedy is contentment. If we are content with our own, we shall not covet that which is another's."

BE CONTENT WITH WHAT YOU HAVE

We arrive now at the middle of the verse and find contentment waiting for us—but with an important difference.

In the previous chapters, Paul gave us two important teachings about contentment: "I have learned the secret of being content" and "godliness with contentment is great gain." It is interesting to note that, in both, he is commending contentment to us, saying, in effect, *contentment is a wonderful and godly way to live, and having found the secret, I recommend it heartily as great gain.*

Now, however, in this Hebrews passage, we find a statement on contentment that binds us to a higher obedience. "Be content with what you have" is not merely a commendation but a commandment. Such a declaration raises the stakes.

When something is *commended* in Scripture, we take notice. God smiles in that direction, which means we walk quickly along the line of His gaze so to remain under His good pleasure. The Spirit has placed these commended words on a hill and cradled them with light that we might be drawn there in good times and bad.

But when something is *commanded* in Scripture, it is of a completely different category. Instead of sitting on a hill, commandments sit atop Mount Sinai. We stand at attention, listen more closely, and realize flexibility is now removed.

To fail a commended verse is foolishness; to fail a commanded verse is sin.

To some this might sound stern, to others, like scare tactics. Personally, when theologian J. I. Packer says, "Contentment is both commended and commanded in Scriptures," I find it helpful. Living in the two realities as we do, so much of God is yet hidden. And it must be so. Despite being surrounded everywhere by abundant evidence, this is still the season of mystery and faith. With His teaching on contentment, however, no ambiguity remains.

We realize now that God wants to blanket us with His protection and shower us with His joy. In giving us the Ten Commandments, the Wisdom Literature, the words of Christ Himself, and now, thrice, the attention of the Epistles with both commendation and commandment, we know for certain this is a treasure buried for the faithful to find. Regardless of the world, we have found the secret of resting under the shadow of the Almighty. His presence will never leave us or forsake us, His provision is enough for our contentment, and His providence will never lapse beneath perfection.

Here are a few prescriptions to help us apply Paul's important words.

Rx: 1   *At All Costs, Avoid Envy*

Envy is a one-way street to misery. It not only dishonors God, but it sets up base camp in our heads and poisons our thoughts. "Envy rots the bones," says Proverbs.[11]

Just because one coworker gets a new pool and another wins the lottery is no reason to hate them. Congratulate them, affirm them, speak kindly to them, for love is patient and kind and does not envy.[12] When we live in grace and goodwill, it is surprising how pleasant life becomes. Ironically, the proud and prosperous often end up envying the contented.

"Where you have envy and selfish ambition, there you find disorder and every evil practice," wrote James. "But the wisdom that comes from heaven is first of all pure; then peace-loving, considerate, submissive, full of mercy and good fruit, impartial and sincere. Peacemakers who sow in peace raise a harvest of righteousness."[13]

Marvin Olasky, the almost impossibly prolific and brilliant editor of *WORLD* magazine, compared his youthful rants as a post-Harvard Jewish communist with his post-conversion life.

> Yes, I know class hatred. A year after graduation, hatred led me into the Communist Party U.S.A. Envy led me to advocate murderous revolution of the kind that ravaged Russia, China, Cuba, Cambodia, and other countries. Envy leads to class warfare. . . . I've written in *WORLD* about how God graciously pulled me out of communism. When I became a Christian in 1976, many of my sinful tendencies

remained. . . . But one instantly disappeared: class envy. Strange but true. My pre-Christian life did not include a day without envy of the rich. My Christian life has not included a day with it.[14]

Rx: 2   *Never Leave God, Never Forsake People*

The phrase *never will I leave you; never will I forsake you* is one of the most beautiful and comforting images of God. Our world is an abandoning kind of place, but God is not that way. Neither are the saints. The story of Thomas Vincent illustrates this well. Vincent, however, was not the only Christian who refused to leave London in perilous times. That description fits the Queen Mum, too.

Many got their first awareness of this remarkable woman as wife of the stammering King George VI in the movie *The King's Speech*. Born in 1900, she came from privilege but was born a commoner. The day she turned fourteen, WWI began. Her family home in Scotland turned into a hospice for the wounded, and she volunteered caring for injured soldiers.

Prince Albert fell in love with her, but she turned down his proposal, "afraid never, never again to be free to think, speak and act as I feel I really ought to." But the prince would marry no one else, and two years later, in 1923, they were wed. It was calm enough until 1936, when Albert's older brother, King Edward VIII, abdicated the throne to marry an American divorcée. In the ensuing constitutional crisis, Albert was crowned king, some say only because Parliament trusted his wife more than him.

Then came WWII.

The people adored their queen and her engaging way with the public. But this popularity soared with her steadfast refusal to leave London during the bombings. Family, friends, and politicians encouraged her to flee to the countryside. She famously answered, "The children won't go without me. I won't leave the King. And the King will never leave." It was an inspirational decision that contributed to her immense reputation for the next sixty years.

Day after day, she traveled to bombed-out portions of the city to comfort the suffering, those who had lost homes or loved ones during the night. She visited hospitals, factories, soldiers, the impoverished East End, and the Docks. She was pleased when Buckingham Palace was damaged in a bombing raid, saying, "I'm glad we've been bombed. It makes me feel I can look the East End in the face."

She was impossibly strong and lifted morale to such a degree that Hitler called her the most dangerous woman in Europe. The King and Queen, both people of faith, called the nation to prayer at critical times and gave public thanks to Almighty God for VE Day. The King died prematurely in 1951, launching their daughter Queen Elizabeth to the throne. The Queen Mother lived another sixty years, dying in 2002 at age 101, always the public's favorite royalty.

The Queen Mum helped plan the funeral to reflect her strong faith. There were readings from Psalms, Revelation, and, at the end, *Pilgrim's Progress*, where Pilgrim nears heaven and his eternal rest. A former Archbishop of Canterbury, Dr. George Carey, said, "She had a deep and sustaining faith and lived her life in the sure and certain hope of the resurrection to eternal life." Billy Graham wrote in his autobiography, "More than anything, the Queen Mother always impressed me with her quiet but firm faith."

Why was this sweet, steadfast Christian Queen so adored? Because she would NEVER leave or forsake those God had given her.

Thomas Vincent and the Queen Mum are but two among untold thousands who have reflected the love of God in this never-forsaking way. Learn from them. Honor them. Become them.

Rx: 3 *Cling to the Word* Never

Certain verses are my favorites on dark days. "Never will I leave you," is one. Think of it—the implications of the word *never*. We say, "I'll pray for you," but we mean it approximately. Same with "Let me know if I can do anything." When we say, "I will now be content," we mean on most days. When God says something, however, it is always backed by precision.

J. C. Ryle (1816–1900) wrote,

> There is a peculiar depth of wisdom in the words, "I will never leave—nor forsake." Observe, God does not say, "My people shall always have pleasant things; they shall always be fed in green pastures, and have no trials—or trials very short and few." He neither says so, nor does He appoint such a lot to His people. On the contrary, He sends them affliction and chastisement. He tries them—by suffering. He purifies them—by sorrow. He exercises their faith—by disappointments. But still, in all these things He promises, "I will never leave—nor forsake."
>
> Let every believer grasp these words, and store them up in his heart. Keep them ready, and have them fresh in your memory; you will need them one day. The Philistines will be upon you; the hand of sickness will lay you low; the king of terror will draw near; the valley of the shadow of death will open up before your eyes. Then comes the hour when you will find nothing so comforting, as a text like this—nothing so cheering, as a realizing sense of God's companionship. Stick to that word "never." It is worth its weight in gold. Cling to it as a drowning man clings to a rope.

Interesting phrase, huh? *The Philistines will be upon you.* I have met them on the road myself. How do we make it through when surrounded? "That is how we endure," wrote the late George Sanchez. "That is how we gain the capacity to persevere. It isn't because of our strength. It isn't because of our commitment. It isn't because we have memorized so many verses. . . . It is because He Himself has said, 'I will never desert you, nor will I ever forsake you.'"[15]

Rx: 4   *Submit to "Be Content"*

God gives a great deal of flexibility on many fronts. Just walk into a Sunday morning service in a hundred countries and you will see what I mean. But when it comes to commandments, such as "be content with what you have," God is a great deal more exacting.

Unfortunately for us, we live in an era of independence, not submission. We are self-contained, self-directed, self-motivated, self-made, self-actualized, self-sufficient, self-assured, and perhaps self-centered, self-indulgent, and self-justifying to boot.

May I make a suggestion? Let us bend the knee in surrender, and may it be a glad surrender. There is one way to joy and peace, and it follows a narrow road. The road belongs to God, but He will share it with us. We won't find contentment unless we agree to "be content" along this path.

A retired physician and spouse left their nice home to enter a retirement apartment. It is a very lovely setting and still a great place for hospitality and ministry. But it lacks the space and other advantages of their home. I asked them if they were content, did they ever wish they had not made the change. "We decided to be content when we came here," they both said together with smiles. "It's cozy, and we decided we like cozy."

Rx: 5 *Keep the Tenth Commandment*

"Do not covet" was a sin when Moses came down the mountain, and it remains a sin today. Coveting is largely internal, more residing in the heart than the hands. It is therefore an important measurement of authenticity before a watching God who ever searches our thoughts and intentions.

"Do not covet" is not as severe as some make it but certainly more than some who underestimate it. Augustine defined covetousness, "to desire more than enough." God does not mind if we wish for a place to live, clothes on our back, a good job, a spouse and children, or a car that works. It is not acceptable, however, to desire things inordinately, to think on them continuously, to be resentful of our neighbor's good fortune, to love the world more than God. The world might fill our eyes but must never get into our hearts. Covetousness, it has been said, chains our hearts to earth.

To faithfully keep the tenth commandment, "Thou shall not covet," will move us well down the line toward a contented life. Still, discontentment is a larger issue than covetousness. For example, if we were a farmer, we might score well by not coveting our neighbor's tractor, herd, or crops. But that still might leave us discontent with the weather. A completely contented farmer would say with Longfellow, "After all, the best thing one can do when it is raining is let it rain."

DO YOU SEE?

We have seen Thomas Vincent's sacrificial faithfulness to seventeenth-century Londoners as an example of God's never forsaking us. Who else would go day after day, ministering house-to-plague-infested-house when it most certainly meant his own death? Vincent, however, was not an island. For instance, he was chosen to be catechist for the highly esteemed John Owen, brilliant church leader and prolific author who preached before Parliament, was vice-chancellor of Oxford, and declined an early presidency of Harvard. Owen is the same who lost eleven of twelve children at young ages, and who wrote concerning contentment:

> Let us be in an expectation of such changes of providence, that they may not be great surprises unto us. When we are in peace, let us look for trouble; when we are at liberty, let us look for restraint; and when our children are about us, let us look for the removal of them; and be content to see all our comforts in their winding-sheet [burial clothes, shroud] every day.

These were stoical times, and contentment needed deep roots. Although Owen failed in his attempts to get John Bunyan (1628–1688) released from prison, when that day came, he offered John the use of his publisher for *Pilgrim's Progress*. The book itself was finished only because of the lengthened prison stay.

Do you see how providence and contentment work together, even in adversity?

As for Bunyan, he was born a poor country boy with limited education who became an itinerant pot mender (tinker) until leaving for the army at age seventeen. Following the English Civil War when another was killed in his place, Bunyan led a reprobate life, married an orphaned young lady, had a blind child, and was "poor as poor might be." His Christian conversion led to his preaching which led to his imprisonment. Yet, despite being incarcerated for twelve years, *Pilgrim's Progress* was for centuries regarded the most read book in the English language after the Bible.

Do you see?

Then there was Nathanael Vincent, three years younger than his brother Thomas, who also went on to be a well-known preacher. Regarding contentment, he wrote,

> Ambition and covetousness after worldly grandeur and gain, which make us so unlike to Christ, should be far from us. If the world be the great thing with us, mammon will have us at command, and Christ will have but little service from us. Why should that be high in the esteem and affection of your hearts, which Christ so little minded?

We might think the pre-progress gloom of 350 years ago has little to do with today. But first let us hear one more account. Before Nico went into the hospital never to return home, Katja and he slept in the same bedroom. They were "teammates." She was four and he eleven months. She adored him.

During the hospitalization, Linda went to help and slept over so Adam and Maureen could be with Nico.

One morning, Katja came running, early as always. "Grandma! Grandma!"

Linda looked up with sleepy eyes and smiled. "Hi Kati. How are you, sweetheart?"

"I just had a dream."

"Oh? What was it about."

"I was sitting in a chair. A man came up to me and I just asked him one word. I said, 'Who are you?'"

Linda got up on her elbow. "What did he say? Who was it?"

"It was Jesus."

Linda propped herself up higher. "That's wonderful, Kati! What happened then?"

"He picked me up and held me."

You see, we are not so very different from the Vincents, Owens, and Bunyans. Children still die, we still grieve, contentment is still needed in good times and bad, and Jesus will never leave us, never forsake us. Especially not four-year-old girls with curly hair who love their brothers so.

CHAPTER 8

CONTENTMENT AND SIMPLICITY

Setting Aside the Things That Hinder

True contentment depends not upon what we have; a tub was large enough for Diogenes, but a world was too little for Alexander.

— C. C. COLTON

Jon's interest in architecture began on his paper route. As he made the rounds, a favorite house always stood out. It belonged to a friendly couple, both architects, and to young Jon it seemed perfect. Not only on the outside, but also when he had a chance to enter for his weekly collections. Although the house was small, it exuded a simple elegance. The heartwarming charm made him look forward to each visit.

As the years passed, the paper route was given to another, and the idyllic image drifted away. Jon entered the university and threw himself into his architecture classes. He created sketches, drawings, and plans, made models, took pictures, collected books and magazines. It was all valuable, everything important — all markers of his progress and accomplishment. His room swelled with clutter until there was barely space to turn around.

By graduation he was happily married to a librarian. They both had good jobs, which means they both made good money, which means they both bought lots of stuff. Not junk, mind you, but sophisticated and expensive objects that represented their professional interests and personal tastes. First it went on walls and shelves and in closets. Then the floor. Then the carport. Boxes were everywhere, stacks were piled high. It was hard to move around, hard to use the kitchen, hard to enjoy being home, hard to have company. Their social life shriveled. They ate out more, saw each other less, came home later, and grew increasingly unhappy.

To compensate, they went on expensive vacations, nice while they lasted but depressing upon return. As the first pregnancy approached term, prospective nannies took one look at the house and immediately refused the job.

About that time, Jon spotted a buried-under-a-pile book on Japanese architecture. He pulled it out and looked at a full-page photo of a residential interior. It instantly reminded him of the small but perfect home he fell in love with years before. "It was like finding a long-lost jewel of enormous value and gave me the direction I needed to help turn our lives around."

When his wife and new baby were visiting grandparents, he went into the bedroom and launched a bold plan that would be either brilliant or catastrophic. He tossed out everything in his closet and bureau that was not used regularly. The walls were swept clear of dozens of pictures and masks. He kept only two photos. The hundreds of books covering one wall were reduced to a dozen and placed in another room, then the bookshelves themselves were taken down. Finally, he painted walls, ceiling, and drawers a very soft blue.

To me, the room was transformed into the space of rest and love it was meant to be. I held my breath when my wife saw it for the first time. What would be her reaction? Heretofore, neither of us had changed anything in our home environment without consulting the other. For a long moment there was total silence. Then she turned to me. There were tears in her eyes. I found out, much to my relief, what they meant when she flung her arms around me.

A garage sale, the local library, and a thrift store took care of the now suddenly "unnecessary" items. Actually, they had five garage sales after duplicating their makeover room to room. "With the transformation of our home, good things began to happen — our bickering and alienation disappeared, our health improved, we spent quality time together, our daughter turned into a delightful little handful, we entertained at home regularly, became gourmet cooks, and found a great nanny."

They put boundaries on work, rarely ate out, skipped expensive trips, paid bills upon arrival, instantly tossed catalogues, and stopped recreational shopping. They purchased nothing that did not first have a specific place to go.[1]

Their joy was restored by simplicity. Their marriage was saved by simplicity. Their lives were revolutionized by simplicity.

CLEARING OUT THE UNDERBRUSH

Every fire season we read how excessive underbrush puts the forest at risk, particularly in drought conditions. Clearing it regularly reduces the risk and restores health to the forest. Similarly, pruning excessive branches leads to a healthier fruit tree and improved harvest.

Our lives are no different. We all need to prune away the excess, to periodically clear out the underbrush: possessions, magazines, books, clothes, furniture, technology, media, information, expectations, decisions. For some this is easy, causing minimal grief. They attack the pile, toss effortlessly, and are done in minutes. For others, well, that is a very different kettle of fish. Whatever the reason, for some of us, it requires a monumental effort to even begin *thinking* about the monumental effort of *beginning* the monumental effort of *throwing* a ten-year-old magazine. Regardless of our personalities and dispositions, it has probably never been more urgent to clear out the clutter. It's all a matter of math.

Simplicity has always been a good idea, but in today's world the stakes are much higher. As already mentioned repeatedly, the mathematics of profusion — *more and more of everything faster and faster* now at exponential rates — has risen to extraordinarily burdensome levels (see the appendix, Dysfunctional Math, on page 211). It works like this. There are more stores and malls for shopping. There are many more online products to be purchased. There are far more ads on far more media platforms, and the ads have a much higher production value enticing more eyes. There are new models of all products, new gadgets for every piece of technology, and new apps (applications) for the best of the best. We have a higher square footage in our houses and fewer people per house, thus more room to stockpile. It is easier than ever to buy, even when in debt. Finally, discontent and coveting feel comfortable in our midst, thus presenting scant challenge to our pursuit of inordinate desires.

When you add it together, the opportunities are up, the restraints are down, and many of us are swimming in it. These are yeasty days for overload. Which also means, of course, that these are important days for simplicity.

As we have learned over the past three decades, going from sufficiency to overload is of no advantage. Overload, by definition, is dysfunctional, which means there are various symptoms associated with it: stress, frustration, disorganization, depression, fatigue, exhaustion, and relational problems. Upon the initial purchase, we experience that familiar tingle followed by the temporary glow of happiness. But after a few days, weeks, or months, the new item is simply assimilated into the growing pile, and it no longer elevates our mood.

WHAT SHOULD I WEAR FOR THE RACE?

Simplicity and contentment are in the same family, more siblings than cousins. Of the two, contentment is the elder. It runs deeper, is more binding and compelling, and has a regal bearing. As we have seen, contentment is commanded and commended in Scripture, and one of the

Ten Commandments is even dedicated to it. I regard it as an elder statesman.

This does not mean, of course, that simplicity suffers from biblical shyness. Both Old and New Testaments endorse the righteous who dedicate their lives to the spiritual over the material. Those who intentionally put limits on their needs and desires, who choose to travel lightly, pivot nimbly, and be unencumbered by excessive attachments, these the Spirit applauds. Just after concluding the hall of fame of faith in Hebrews 11, we find this verse: "Therefore, since we are surrounded by such a great cloud of witnesses, let us throw off everything that hinders and the sin that so easily entangles. And let us run with perseverance the race marked out for us."[2] The phrase *let us throw off everything that hinders* (elsewhere translated "let us also lay aside every encumbrance" [NASB] or "let us strip off every weight that slows us down" [NLT]) is one of the guiding principles of my life.

When we speak of spiritual disciplines, contentment is an internal discipline (such as prayer, fasting, meditation), while simplicity is an external discipline (such as service, giving, worship). Contentment is on the inside, of the heart and spirit, and yes, the head as well. "Contentment is," writes Jeremiah Burroughs, "a sweet, inward heart thing. It is a work of the Spirit indoors." Simplicity, on the other hand, is on the outside, often the working out of contentment in the world.

There is a completely natural relationship between being content and living simply. I can hardly think of the one without the other. Being inwardly content means we don't need or desire to be surrounded by any particular level of outward adornment. Biblical contentment whispers constantly, and very sweetly I might add, that it is not about the house, car, degree, or bank account, or, for that matter, the hair or height or nose. It is nice, of course, to have a house and bank account and nose, but these are merely add-ons, useful tools, never to be thought of as a central focus of existence.

There is an old Indian proverb, "By sitting in a golden cage, no crow becomes a swan." In the same way, no outward adornment can accomplish what God wishes for us, because the outside is not His primary target. He always works deep. He wants us to be swans, not crows faking it in golden cages.

Here are some prescriptions to help us on the journey. You will notice, even in this small sampling, how inclusive the partnership of simplicity and contentment is. There are few areas in our lives that are not touched by these biblical principles.

Rx: 1   *Stay Off the Hedonic Treadmill*

Studies have shown that economically developed countries do not have higher levels of happiness than less-developed countries. For decades, we have gained in education, earned more money, and bought more expensive houses. Then we filled our homes to the rafters with endless bounty. Our national fixation with *more* has been very successful. Yet, somehow, our overall emotional well-being has not improved.

Let's say, for example, that happiness is measured on a scale of 0 to 100, and our current level is 70. If we reach a life goal, get a promotion, receive a pay raise, or acquire a new car, our level might rise to 85. The problem is, it doesn't remain there. Before long, it predictably drops back to the baseline of 70.

In order to get back to 85, we repeat the process. Perhaps we find an even better job, but this one requires more hours and stress. We move to the suburbs to buy a bigger house, but it increases our commute. We buy more possessions that soon feel like clutter. Our score keeps rising, then falling back. Psychologists and economists call this cycle a hedonic (pleasure-related) treadmill. As the speed and elevation keep increasing, we must run faster and faster to stay in the same place.

There appears to be an invisible stabilization factor, a happiness set point, at work within individuals and societies. In part, this explains why our *pursuit of more* in the West has not been accompanied by an increase in overall life satisfaction. Futurists in the 1960s thought we would trade the money gained by increased productivity for more time off and higher pursuits. We didn't. We stayed on the hedonic treadmill and now have such expensive lives that we find ourselves trapped. Another factor to consider: progress gives us more material benefits, but (as explained in my book *Margin*) it also leads to increasing stress, change, complexity, speed, intensity, imbalance, and overload.

In the end, we sacrificed the many advantages of simplicity but did not gain in happiness, joy, satisfaction, or contentment. For millions, this has been a heavy price to pay. Isaiah's question applies well for all of us on the treadmill, "Why spend money on what is not bread, and your labor on what does not satisfy?"[3]

Rx: 2 *Listen to the Past*

I am aware of the problem of romanticizing the past but even more aware of our tendency toward chronological arrogance. Yes, we have more education, information, communication, and technology than our ancestors. But wisdom? Depth? Simplicity? I doubt it. We moderns are a superficial, twitching, distracted people, and it is good for us to sit at the feet of our elders and hear their words.

C. S. Lewis defined chronological snobbery as "the uncritical assumption that whatever has gone out of date is on that account discredited."[4] When it comes to contentment, voices from the past seem more reflective, and you have undoubtedly noticed throughout the book how extensively I refer to them. Our ancestors possessed a greater wealth of experience with gritty, life-and-death suffering and its opportunities for contentment amidst the pain and depravity of daily life. Personally, I draw inspiration from their words and strength from their example.

When tragedy strikes today, we rage against the person perceived responsible. In the past, committed believers referred their suffering and tragedy to the throne of God and His providence. Even though this approach has "gone out of date," it is more comforting to the human soul than filing litigious grievances.

In previous writings, I introduced readers to a remarkable frontier woman named Elinore Pruitt Stewart. After being widowed, she traveled from Colorado to Wyoming to work for a rancher, then later became his wife. One hundred years ago, in 1913, *Letters of a Woman Homesteader* was first published. The loss of her first son, baby Jamie, was especially painful. Elinore wrote poignantly about the sad pleasure of being able to do the things needed for burial preparations and internment. Then she continued,

> Little Jamie was the first little Stewart. God has given me two more precious little sons. The old sorrow is not so keen now. I can bear to tell you about it, but I never could before. When you think of me, you must think of me as one who is truly happy. It is true, I want a great many things I haven't got, but I don't want them enough to be discontented and not enjoy the many blessings that are mine. I have my home among the blue mountains, my healthy, well-formed children, my clean, honest husband, my kind gentle milk cows, my garden which I make myself. I have loads and loads of flowers which I tend myself. There are lots of chickens, turkeys, and pigs which are my own special care. I have some slow old gentle horses and an old wagon. I can load up the kiddies and go where I please any time. I have the best, kindest neighbors and I have my dear absent friends. Do you wonder I am so happy? When I think of it all, I wonder how I can crowd all my joy into one short life.[5]

Who talks like this today? No one I know. *Do you wonder I am so happy? When I think of it all, I wonder how I can crowd all my joy into one short life.*

If we wish to learn the secret of contentment, listen to those who went before. Their experiences and stories have not gone out of date. They have the capacity to nurture our souls, strengthen our simplicity, and enrich our contentment. It is little wonder C. S. Lewis advised us to read frequently outside our own century.

Rx: 3   *Don't Grow the Pile, Throw It*

Possessions pile up. Clutter mounts. Acquisitions happen. Stuff has an expanding mind of its own. These things are like lawns—they just keep growing.

In these hyperdynamic times, most of us do not need to invite clutter into our homes. We wake up each morning, and there it is. It comes in the night, sneaks in while we are sleeping and makes itself at home. Before you can blink, it has taken over the guest bedroom. Then the basement and garage.

Many of our houses have nonstop conveyor belts coming into side windows filled with boxes, blouses, bags, toys, tools, and tutus. These marvelous items come from just about everywhere. Some come from stores, including my favorite, Fleet Farm. Some from the mailman or UPS or FedEx. Some from grandparents, friends, and neighbors. Some arrive courtesy of Internet sales, Craigslist, or eBay. A person today does not even require green money to acquire clutter; coins can get the job done. With garage sales, thrift shops, and dollar stores, endless mounds are available for all comers.

Each day, each week, the pile either increases or decreases. In today's world, there is no such thing as staying the same. We have two choices: Grow it or throw it.

At some point, we need to confront our stuff, and a "clutter buddy" can help. Announce it on social media to increase accountability. Turn off the conveyor belt. Better yet, reverse the direction of the conveyor belt and bless your neighbors with some.

Intentionally diminish the shopping choices rather than expand them. Throw out the catalogues, unless we want to turn our houses into shopping malls.

The result is the blessing of simplicity restored, with a nice side order of peace and contentment. We now have the opportunity of enjoying each remaining possession much more. Simplicity can cut our pile in half but double our contentment.

Rx: 4   *Beware of Impulses*

A recent study reported that 76 percent of a shopper's purchasing decisions were made in the store. This represents a new high for this kind of survey.[6] There are many reasons for such elevated numbers: seductive packaging, in-store displays, specials the shopper was unaware of, the huge number of products in stores (40,000 in the average supermarket, 150,000 for a Walmart superstore), popular impulse items near checkout counters. "What you find is that people will tell you they plan to do one thing, but their actual behavior will be quite different," said the president of a marketing association.[7] In other words, we are not that hard to manipulate.

If you were walking down a concourse at the airport and delicious smells came wafting out of three stores, which would you choose—cinnamon buns, barbeque, or chocolate? Each is famously alluring, making you hungry for the product even if you are not. Now imagine an entire world filled with the visual equivalent. It is little wonder impulse shopping is such a temptation.

Simplicity is about intentionality and boundary formation, the opposite of impulse shopping. Simplicity is about priority-based decision making, frugality, and consumer restraint, not random and expensive impulses. Simplicity is about being content with less, with enough, with sufficiency. Last-minute revisions while shopping will usually take more time, cost more money, and bring home unwanted clutter and calories.

To put this in a positive light, such situations give us the opportunity to exercise the discipline of simplicity each time we enter a store. This is God gently shaking our cage. He wants us to seek first His kingdom rather than a "seductively packaged" item that suddenly strikes our fancy. It is but a small test, yet important enough to matter. He is pulling us away, equipping us for something much higher than our impulses.

Rx: 5 *Try One Step at a Time*

Sobriety is best accomplished one step at a time. Sometimes that is the best approach for simplicity as well. Perhaps one room at a time, similar to Jon's story. Or one closet at a time. Or one drawer at a time. Or one habit at a time.

It was not easy for Jon. Behaviors, habits, precedents, and patterns such as these are developed over many years and are not easy to dislodge. Every item might have a memory attached, or perhaps be a gift intended. For some people, the attachment to various items is extraordinarily strong. Accumulations often connect to deep-seated needs in our spirit.

These are not random impulses as much as obsessions, and obsessions are never easy.

For other people, it is simply a matter of inertia. The problem is too big, I'll tackle it tomorrow. I don't have time. Or energy. I need to floss my teeth. Again.

Once the process is started, the results are hopefully self-sustaining. I know of people who have quite nice homes that are rendered nearly unusable by clutter. Once hospitality begins again, once family and friends can sleep over again, once opening a cupboard is no longer a dysfunctional event, once lost items easily resurface, the blessings of space and simplicity might combine to form a new reality of freedom and contentment.

Rx: 6 *Consider Dying Like Your Doctor*

Dr. Ken Murray, a recently retired family physician once affiliated with USC, wrote an article titled "How Doctors Die: It's Not Like the Rest of Us, but It Should Be."[8] The piece went viral, ricocheting across the nation and touching off an overwhelmingly positive discussion. The article is more anecdotal than scientific but based on a lifetime of experience and observation.

It turns out that many (if not most) medical professionals react to their own terminal diagnosis with resigned simplicity. Knowing precisely what they face, these doctors refuse to put themselves through the agony and expense of heroic measures. One highly respected orthopedist found a lump in his abdomen that was diagnosed as aggressive cancer. "He went home the next day, closed his practice, and never set foot in a hospital again. He focused on spending time with family and feeling as good as possible. Several months later, he died at home. He had no chemotherapy, radiation, or surgical treatment. Medicare didn't spend much on him."

It is not hypocritical for these same physicians to explain possible life-extending measures to patients who wish to hear all the options. But doctors know better about what comes next. "The patient will get cut open, perforated with tubes, hooked up to machines, and assaulted with drugs. All of this occurs in the Intensive Care Unit at a cost of tens of thousands of dollars a day. What it buys is misery we would not inflict on a terrorist." This may be the more extreme end of the spectrum, but the point is still valid. Such measures gain some patients a few months, but most doctors are determined to avoid this kind of experience in their own final days.

Patients are in a vulnerable position, shocked by the diagnosis and frightened by impending death. Family members, too, are reeling and at times hysterical. It is understandable they should hope for a few extra months and perhaps even reach for a miracle cure. Sitting on the other side, doctors have the advantage of good clinical instincts informed by extensive experience. They "sense" how this is going to turn out. It's fine if the patient chooses such last-ditch options in the face of a fatal diagnosis, but for themselves? No thanks. Seen it too often.

Is this melancholic fatalism on their part? No. Simply a desire to control a very important interval of their lives — that span between today and the end.

The medical system is wondrous in many ways, and today we have so many more tools to fight cancer, to push it back. The judgment and timing is therefore important, and, of course, these are intensely personal decisions. However, when the disease is aggressive, when metastases are widespread, when medical statistics are grim, when the heart is gone, or the brain is not firing, then heaven is knocking and Jesus is waiting.

It is at such times the medical system can become a monster, a runaway train, sucking money out of our pockets and time out of our days. In addition, the results are often socially isolating, keeping us from the support we need most. As the costs escalate, the train just keeps chugging ahead, one painful intervention after another. Patients feel trapped by a life-or-death process, afraid to "quit in the middle" yet equally afraid to continue.

"Almost anyone can find a way to die in peace at home," says Dr. Murray, "and pain can be managed better than ever. Hospice care, which focuses on providing terminally ill patients with comfort and dignity rather than on futile cures, provides most people with much better final days. Amazingly, studies have found that people placed in hospice care often live longer than people with the same disease who are seeking active cures."

As if to prove the point, Dr. Murray mentions his older cousin, Torch. He had a seizure which tests confirmed to be lung cancer spread to the brain. Murray opened his home to Torch and they had a wonderful time reconnecting, visiting Disneyland, and watching sports on TV. Eight months later (twice as long as predicted), Torch lapsed into a coma and died. Total cost for medical care during this time was $20.

This article does not mention the faith factor, but for me, faith informs everything. And, quite honestly, I find faith an even stronger reason to support this argument. I have no intention of allowing the end of my life to be dominated by medical, governmental, and financial institutions. My plan, if this situation ever arises, is to turn to the institutions of family and faith. I trust God with my life. I trust God with my death. Why would I not trust God with my dying?

The simplicity-in-dying discussion effortlessly extends to simplicity in funerals. Mine will be uncomplicated and inexpensive (as already described in *In Search of Balance*, "Taking Back Your Funeral"[9]). I have no particular animosity toward funeral directors, doctors, or hospitals, and many I know are marvelous and commendable. I do protest, however, an *overall system* that has escalated the costs and complexities of health care, dying, and funerals without mercy.

Fortunately, we can do much to regain a measure of control, especially if we are willing to walk the path of simplicity and contentment. At a funeral not long ago, it was said of the man, "He lived well, but he died even better." A wonderful eulogy in eight words, fit for a saint.

Rx: 7   *Throw Off Everything That Hinders*

This wonderful but underused biblical phrase deserves our attention if we want to experience simple, contented living. The phrase is appropriately sandwiched between two strong images. Before it is an impressive cloud of faithful witnesses, saints and martyrs who walked uprightly and paid dearly. Immediately after is the image of Christ, the author and perfecter of our faith who scorned the suffering of the cross.

We are placed between these towering inspirations, and our instructions are to walk in the footsteps of the saints while fixing our gaze on Jesus. This is serious business but of the joyous sort. God wants us to engage the task with relish, removing obstacles in the way of a biblically obedient life, sweeping aside the trash in the path, throwing off the clutter, laying down the backpacks filled with worldly preoccupations. Anything we see that distracts us inordinately or that tempts us to wander off the path of authenticity should be removed—anything that blocks our view of Jesus, for it is in looking unto Him that we "will not grow weary and lose heart."[10]

THINGS THAT HINDER

What hinders us? What distracts us? In what ways does the Evil One corrupt us "from the simplicity that is in Christ"?[11] There is a long smorgasbord to choose from, and here is a sampling.

TV, Movies—For some, it is television or movies, spending too much time and seeing violent or sexual images that hinder us and do damage to our spirits. If it hinders, set it aside.

Facebook—Even as social media connects us to acquaintances, it can also lead to addictive use, snatch away huge swaths of our time, and cause Facebook envy. Our friends mean no harm when they post photos of their new cars, perfect kids, and far-away vacations in exotic places. Still, it is sometimes hard to be pleased for them if we are stuck at home with no money, no time, and whiny toddlers. Don't get angry, don't envy. Just bless your friends, and then set aside Facebook if it hinders.

One young lady did exactly that. She heard me at a conference, and then went home and made a few changes. She wrote (with gratitude) that by stopping two things—Facebook and texting—she gained one and a half hours a day. Wow. That was easy.

Judging—Judging others is a hindrance with several simultaneous victims: not only those we condemn with our thoughts and words but also ourselves. To judge another becomes a self-inflicted wound. It is best to presume our incompetence in such matters, keep our hearts within the domain of love, and leave the judgment to God.

Aging—Oh, how we rage against aging today and push it far beyond simplicity and contentment. In previous eras, the elderly received special respect. Name the topic, and they were the wisest, the most experienced. No longer. For this and other reasons, many furiously fight getting older. Eventually, however, we all lose the war with wrinkles, brain cramps, and sagging body parts. A simplicity approach suggests aging with grace. To be content with our chronological status is a pretty straightforward argument, and it saves money and anxiety. In addition, aging gracefully is quite attractive in ways this world knows little of.

Thoughts, Words—Some of us hinder our spiritual lives by thinking too much, others by talking too much. Is it possible to simplify our thoughts, to slow our words, or even to shut them down for a brief fast? Any behavior can be modified at least to some degree. Maturity is the process of diminishing our weaknesses and fortifying our strengths.

Many of us think too much about things that cannot be changed, about things that went wrong, about embarrassing events in our past, about worries for the future, and about "if onlys" and "what ifs." None of this is helpful. "Misery," said the French moralist Joseph Joubert (1754–1824), "is almost always the result of thinking." One hundred years earlier, English essayist Joseph Addison wrote, "A contented mind is the greatest blessing a man can enjoy in this world."

Other people can't stop talking and thus exhaust themselves and everyone within twenty feet. Proverbs says to "avoid anyone who talks too much."[12] Paul adds, "Make it your ambition to lead a quiet life."[13] Dallas Willard says that "silence involves two things: quiet and not talking." Isaiah writes: "In quietness and trust is your strength."[14]

Though an introvert, I am verbal and my brain is a poorly-controlled explosion. Even I need a break from that. Simplicity in thought and word suggests that a quiet mind and a quiet tongue might be enough to coax contentment back into the room.

Comparisons—The comparison game is a hindrance for almost all of us. It is malignant. It distracts us from simplicity, from contentment, and from Christ. Part of the problem is we compare up. We see people who have more, land good jobs, have beautiful families, and seemingly have few problems. So, just as the young lady stopped Facebook, perhaps we should stop comparing. We'll be happier if we grant grace to all, are excited about the good fortune of others, and always spread goodwill.

Perhaps our comparison should be to Christ rather than to peers. He had few if any possessions yet was content. He saw the rich but never envied them. His friends had settled down with families, and, of course, Jesus loved children but remained single. He was brilliant but worked with His hands until the last few years, never begrudging manual labor. He had access to power but did not use it for selfish gain. He was abused but taught blessing to those who persecute us. He lived to thirty-three, while we live to eighty. He was born with nothing, lived with nothing, died with nothing.

Paul said, "Have this attitude in yourselves which was also in Christ Jesus," and then explains how Jesus "emptied Himself nothing," took on the "form of a bond-servant," and "humbled Himself."[15] Understand, Jesus does not want us to torch our possessions in one big bonfire . . . except, maybe, in our hearts.

GIVING THANKS IN THE HOLLOW

Autumn stretched a banner across the Appalachian hills announcing the coming of Thanksgiving. Among her "mountain-folk neighbors" of West Virginia, Sister Bridget Haase shared life and heart, and the sharing went both ways.

One evening an old truck carrying Delena and Elam pulled up. "We'd be rightly honored if you would join us for Thanksgiving dinner," they said. "You're a long way from home, and it's a family day. We're asking early 'cuz we'd like to plan."

It was a kind invitation but delivered with hesitation. The impoverished family, including five children, lived deep in a hollow accessible only by an impossible mud road, seldom traveled.

Sister Bridget said with a smile that she would be delighted. "Bring nothing," Elam said. "Nothing at all."

Thanksgiving was cold but without snow. Sister Bridget arrived at the ramshackle house to find it without water, plumbing, or electricity. A coal stove heated only a single room. Sections of cardboard were taped together forming walls to encircle the family and hold in heat. The children, oblivious to poverty, were overjoyed at the guest and squealed their excitement.

Standing around the table, they held hands and gave fervent thanks for their blessings and then they sat. Sister noticed she had the best plate, a Mason jar glass, a spoon, and a fork. The family of seven shared the other two plates, two Mason jars, and three forks.

The cardboard was decorated with pine cones and fir branches and the message "A big welcome to the church lady." Elam offered a plate of some sort of challenging meat covered with oil. "Good, strong, wild meat," he said without further qualification. Delena then handed over the last of the greens and some mushrooms. Soon dinner was laced with laughing and the rousing singing of "The Old Rugged Cross." Before anyone could notice, it was dusk.

Delena grabbed Sister's hand. "We have somethin' to say before you leave. Hain't never, I mean never, has anyone done come to our home to eat with us. Not that we hain't invited them. But you came. And you came on Thanksgiving." She paused. "No, it wasn't you. Today Jesus himself done come to our home, and we give thanks for the blessing of his presence. We look upon him."[16]

Thanksgiving is not what we have made it, nor is hospitality. These things are not about turkey, fancy china, or cutlery, really, although those are nice. Thanksgiving and hospitality are simpler than that. Just as life is simpler. How shall we dress, then, for the race set out before us? "Clothe yourselves with compassion, kindness, humility, gentleness and patience."[17]

When simplicity and contentment are active across the widest range of human experience, when all are invited to the party, then we know the kingdom is very near.

CHAPTER 9

CONTENTMENT AND MONEY

A Different Kind of Wealth

He is rich or poor according to what he is, not according to what he has.

— Henry Ward Beecher

Chinnapayan Krishnan is a rat exterminator in southern India. His people, a small untouchable caste called the Irula, have traditionally been rat and snake catchers for local farmers, providing an invaluable service. To accomplish his work, Krishnan searches for tunnels and then blocks up all the exits except one. Next, he puts a clay pot over the open hole, starts a fire, and blows smoke into the burrow. Before long, the rodent is stunned. Krishnan reaches in, finds the tail, and extracts the creature blindly.

In the past, these practices yielded five rats a day, and Krishnan was paid five cents each. Recently, however, a new invention arrived, a metal container to house the fire with an attached air pump. The increased efficiency allows him to harvest twenty rats per day, quadrupling his daily income—finally up to the vaunted dollar-a-day level. But that's not all. He brings these critters home to his family that includes nine kids. Add in the grain scraped out of the lair, and voila, they have all they need for their once daily meal.

His hut is small, the walls are mud, the floor is dirt, and the roof is straw. But at least now they have plenty of food. "My children don't go hungry these days," he said, handing the catch to his wife. "They feast."

Since Krishnan's photo first surfaced some years ago in a news weekly, I have not been able to get him out of my thoughts. Looking now for the hundredth time, I've memorized every part of the picture. A poor man kneels on the ground dressed in a white sleeveless T-shirt and a pair of white shorts. With his left hand, he holds up a listless rodent and smiles proudly.

Two things entrance me about this man—the rat he holds by the tail and his Mona Lisa smile. I have looked at that rat so often that we are now friends. As for Krishnan's smile, it is not actually because of the rat. He is smiling because of his new-found wealth.

Here is an intriguing question: At the time someone took this picture, just as my new Indian friend was earning 400 percent more, was he a happier man than I was? When he started bringing home plenty of meat and grain and when the new rat trap gave "a sense of hope to our community that we, too, can have productive lives,"[1] during that particular interval of time, did he have a deeper sense of contentment than I?

It is an interesting question for us in the West to ponder. Sounds preposterous, doesn't it, to even consider such a notion, that an impoverished untouchable living on mangy rats might be "happier" than a successful middle-class American.

What contributes to our sense of joy and satisfaction? Do the countries with the most money have the most happiness? Do the countries with the most progress have the most contentment? Does a heightened socioeconomic level automatically increase our satisfaction with life?

"INDIANS AMONG HAPPIEST ON PLANET"

Linda and I lived in India for three months while working for a small mission hospital decades ago. We love India. We have Indian friends, enjoy Indian food, and display miscellaneous memorabilia. We even speak a few words of Hindi. As a futurist and trends watcher, I follow the country closely. It has risen rapidly to the status of a truly global player. India's middle class is as large as the entire U.S. population, it has millions of highly educated professionals, and it is the world's largest democracy.

Of course, there are negatives as well: poverty, malnourished children, illiteracy, corruption, religious persecution, regional ethnic conflict, public health, and pollution among them. Nevertheless, progress continues even if at times unevenly.

It might come as a surprise that, at least during the time period of a recent survey, India ranked as the second happiest country in the world. Granted, this Ipsos survey included only twenty-four representative countries, but among those polled, Indonesia was first (51 percent very happy), followed by India (43 percent very happy), Mexico, Brazil, Turkey, and then the U.S. (28 percent very happy).[2] (Ipsos identifies the *very happy* category as the most important measurement for accurate comparison because it identifies the depth and intensity of happiness.)

The majority in the affluent West automatically assume that we are the happiest because we are the wealthiest. Of all the eras in history, we have it the best, and so, obviously, our mood must reflect that. Hmmm, on second thought, perhaps not. The results of this poll, typical for such surveys, show the U.S. tied for sixth, not a bad position. But most would be surprised to find Indonesia, India, Mexico, and Turkey ahead of us, with Indonesia nearly doubling the U.S. score.

Let's look at another country, Nigeria. It is my index country for Africa, the most populous country on the continent and a major world oil producer. It is also chronically besieged by chaotic political and economic problems, as well as fighting between Muslims and Christians. Where do they fit on the happiness surveys? A British study of sixty-five countries within the past decade placed them at the top. Immediately following Nigeria was Mexico, Venezuela, El Salvador, and Puerto Rico. The U.S. was sixteenth.[3]

It turns out that, despite frequent chaos, Nigerian people are famous for their optimism, smiles, and laughter. A Nigerian teacher in Minnesota told me he had never met a depressed Nigerian. We personally have known scores of Nigerians—some extremely well—and all fit the pattern.

Let's set aside the happiness issue for a moment and look at another type of study on *Quality of Life*. This report includes 188 countries.[4] Here, as expected, Western nations finish at or near the top, with the U.S. at number one. Listed below are all the countries mentioned in the previous few paragraphs along with their quality of life rankings.

Quality of Life Rankings for 188 Countries

U.S.	1
Mexico	39
Brazil	43
Turkey	67
El Salvador	77
Indonesia	99
Puerto Rico	100
India	138
Venezuela	145
Nigeria	162

We quickly see a disconnect between Happiness and Quality of Life rankings. Nigeria finished 1st in the happiness survey but 162nd in the quality of life study; Indonesia was 1st in the happiness survey but 99th in the quality of life study; and India was 2nd in the happiness survey but 138th in the quality of life study.

It seems the happiness of a nation has less to do with its quality of life than we might think. For many of us, this is a pretty jarring thought. On the other hand, it is nice to be reassured that God does not preferentially give joy only to the economically advantaged.

MONEY DOES NOT BUY HAPPINESS, EXCEPT . . .

On a *global scale*, if happiness is our goal, it is clear that affluent countries have no advantage. The GDP (gross domestic product) per capita in the U.S. is twenty times higher than in Nigeria,[5] but we are less happy than they are. Every study confirms this same general result. The desire for material acquisition functions as a happiness suppressant. When short-term mission doctors return from such countries, they always comment on the surprising happiness of very poor people.

On a *chronological scale*, people across the ages have always found their own sources of happiness, and to assume moderns have a degree of joy unknown to previous generations is presumptuous. For example, studies across industrialized countries have found no increase in happiness from WWII until the present despite greatly increased wealth. You will remember Mrs. Stewart writing to us from Wyoming a hundred years ago about a joy with life she could hardly contain.

Within the U.S., on an *internal scale*, here we find our emotions tracking more in line with common perceptions. People show increasing happiness with increasing income up to the point when we can afford our perceived basic needs. This result is fairly self-evident in that the chronic stress of meeting monthly bills is very painful, and falling behind month after month is hard to endure. After the point where our basic needs are met, happiness levels out. Beyond this level, with further rising of income we do experience an increase in "overall life satisfaction" but also an offsetting increase in worry, anxiety, work pressures, and aggravation.[6]

HAPPINESS VERSUS CONTENTMENT: MUST WE FIGHT?

This book, obviously, is about contentment, but I personally view contentment as a member of a family that includes happiness, joy, and satisfaction. Not everyone, however, is happy about happiness. This is a good time to clarify.

First of all, happiness has lots of press, much more than contentment. There are thousands of studies and surveys on happiness, thousands of books on the subject, and tens of thousands of articles. Harvard has a continuing happiness study that goes back seventy-five years, and there is even a *Journal of Happiness Studies*.

In economics, a quasi specialty branch now exists called Happiness Economics. In politics, the prime minister of the United Kingdom instructed his government to compile a Happiness Index to guide public policy development. The golden moment in the politics of happiness came when Thomas Jefferson crafted a remarkable sentence into our Declaration of Independence. "We hold these truths to be self-evident, that all men are created equal, that they are endowed by their Creator with certain unalienable Rights, that among these are Life, Liberty and the pursuit of Happiness." It is one of the most famous sentences in the history of governance, and rightly so.

Some people, however, object to all this happiness talk. Happiness is a flighty thing, changeable, they say. We are happy one day, grumpy the next. It all depends on the circumstances at the time — maybe our hormones, how much sleep we got, the weather, or how our favorite sports team is playing.

Kirsty Young, forty-three, a British television personality, agrees. "I don't want my children to be 'happy,'" she said. "They will be bloody lucky if they glimpse it now and again. I want them to be content and have self-worth." Even though her husband is a multimillionaire, Ms. Young's own childhood was difficult and she feels it is important to struggle through with hard work and self-discipline. Many voice support for her comments — but not all.

"She is totally and profoundly wrong," said Anthony Seldon,

cofounder of a British political group campaigning for a happiness agenda. "I feel sorry for her children. Every parent should want their child to be happy more than anything else in life, to achieve that sense of deep fulfillment, that they are experiencing life to the full." Seldon is also master at Wellington College, in the forefront of teaching students about happiness. "It is all about psychological health, about connectedness and engagement, about relationships, doing good, appreciating nature and art. Happiness underpins them all. At a time when we are experiencing so much mental illness, teaching youngsters about happiness enables them to see what they can be and to strive for it."

He did not stop there but instead launched an artillery barrage at Young's regard for contentment. "To me, contentment is . . . passive and subservient. As a teacher, I spend my life making young people discontented so they can maximize their lives."[7]

Wow. Must we fight? How ironic that such heated rhetoric develops over two such pleasant words: contentment and happiness.

Sometimes, before we know it, our viewpoints become unnecessarily rigid and we find ourselves defending awkward positions. If we don't want happiness, does this mean we prefer everyone to be unhappy? If we don't believe in contentment, do we realize we've wandered into dangerous theological territory?

Obviously, much of this controversy is about definitions. When all the arguments are peeled back, perhaps people will discover more common ground than initially recognized. Maybe we want approximately the same thing but just don't know it.

For example, when Kirsty Young rails against happiness, no doubt she is speaking about the most superficial and hedonistic tendencies associated with that word. When our children's upbringing is totally dedicated to happiness, we risk turning them into narcissists, little divas and emperors who think the world owes them a continuous river of happiness. We should want our children to experience a measure of the discipline and suffering in life that will make them deeper and more compassionate people.

On the other hand, Mr. Seldon's disdain for contentment is surely referring to laziness, sloth, indolence, and indifference. No passion, no enthusiasm, no creativity. Students who don't care about anything, who are apathetic, disengaged, with no goals or vision.

Attempts at clear definitions of happiness and contentment will be challenged by both sides. But perhaps we should just lower the decibels enough to say each is helpful and even desirable within the scope of realistic commonsense definitions.

Both are gifts — Contentment and happiness, rightly understood, are both gifts from God. Contentment is a strongly biblical notion, as we have seen throughout this book. Happiness, too, is found throughout the Scriptures, and together with the related words rejoice, glad, gladness, joy, joyful, joyous, joyfully, we find hundreds of mentions.

People who are happy with a cheery disposition are winsome. They draw other people to them. They advertise the kingdom well. They have more friends, fewer diseases, and live longer. Given that God made four-year-olds laugh every four minutes is a signal to the rest of us — don't take ourselves so seriously. Let me put it this way — on a cross-country flight, would you rather sit next to a happy child or an unhappy one? Would you rather be married to a happy spouse or an unhappy one?

Both overlap — Contentment and happiness are not the same, but there are areas of overlap. The kind of happiness I am most interested in is the kind that intersects with contentment. Jonathan Edwards (1703–1758) wrote a remarkable essay titled "Full Contentment in Christ"[8] in which he uses the words contentment/content fourteen times and happiness/happy twenty-seven times.

One surface, the other deep — Happiness is more a surface emotion and thus more related to mood and feelings. In the same way the surface of the sea may be smooth or agitated, the surface of a person can reveal a lot about how they are feeling at that moment. Contentment, on the other hand, is deeper and more related to character. If we dive far enough beneath the surface of the sea, the water is calm. In the same way, contentment is more unchanging, more dependable, and also more spiritually significant.

In another analogy, happiness is like the *weather* that can change daily, even hourly. It is sunny and warm at noon, but dark and stormy at supper—just like our mood. Contentment is more like the *climate*. Perhaps we feel it is impossible to change either the weather or the climate. Actually, we can change both. Just move. If we do not like rainy weather, we can pack up our things and move to a drier climate. This is precisely what the Bible tells us to do about contentment. If we are not content, we can change our character by moving closer to Christ.

CONTENTMENT AND MONEY: A CONFLICTED STORY

Why all the fuss about money? It seems there should be a matter-of-factness to the subject. It is, after all, simply a medium of exchange. We can't eat green paper, nor for that matter, silver or gold. Money is just a placeholder, making it easier to buy, sell, accumulate, store, and manage an economy. A dollar is worth only what the international markets say it is worth. Since we must have something as a medium of exchange, what is the big deal?

God understood the importance of this issue from the beginning. The Scriptures paint two very contrasting pictures about money. On the righteous side, God uses money to bless untold millions and advance the kingdom. On the unrighteous side, the Evil One uses money to corrupt people, to separate them from God and each other, and to sow discord and discontent. In the battleground of good versus evil, there has never been a force as powerful as money.

The following is a brief summary of the spiritual pros and cons. It is important to note that God never, under any conditions, *needs* money to accomplish His purposes. That said, He does *use* money in various ways to bless His people and also to test us.

The Blessing of Money

Money has the opportunity to bring great good and spread blessing when it is used wisely, generously, and biblically.

- God gives us the ability to earn money, just as He gives us the ability to work and provide for our needs.
- Money allows us to obtain a place to live and pay our expenses.
- Money allows us to purchase the unprecedented advantages of progress, including not only necessities but many comforts and desires as well.
- Money allows us to have experiences denied earlier generations, traveling being one example.
- Money allows us the joy of experiencing that "It is more blessed to give than to receive."[9]
- Money allows us to test our hearts to see if we are funnels or sponges.
- Money allows more businesses to grow and hire, allowing more people to live better and give more.
- Money is used for the growth of the local church and other community ministries.
- Money sponsors unprecedented, explosive mission work around the world.
- As God determines, He gives significant wealth to righteous people for the benefit of building up the church and providing for the poor.
- God anoints some with the "gift of giving," blessing such givers with resources and linking them directly to people and organizations in need.

The Curse of Money

Money has been used for millennia as a medium of commercial exchange, but since the Industrial Revolution, it has picked up speed and gained in dominance. Today, it flies around the globe at unheard-of speeds and basically combines with progress to run the world. The Bible warns us repeatedly about its power, speaking more about money than prayer.

Money is singled out by God for special warning. It is the only power having the audacity to go toe to toe with God and challenge Him for ownership. "No one can serve two masters," Jesus said. "Either you will hate the one and love the other, or you will be devoted to the one and despise the other. You cannot serve both God and money."[10]

- Money has now replaced God in the hearts of many. If as a nation we love money more than God, He will notice. "You may say to yourself, 'My power and the strength of my hands have produced this wealth for me.' But remember the LORD your God, for it is he who gives you the ability to produce wealth."[11]
- Money and progress now have autonomous power. Together, they control our economy, which means they control our institutions, government, and individual lives.
- The economic and financial systems are very complex and tightly coupled. They are increasingly too big to fail and too big to bail.
- Economics is the new sacred domain: It gets what it needs. If you try to touch it, you will get both hands cut off.
- Money belongs to a dangerous quartet: money, sex, power, fame.
- Money leads to addictive behavior.
- Money has led to a work, earn, and spend cycle. Each time around the track, the *spend* is greater than the *earn*, thus requiring more *work*.
- The requirement for more money keeps accelerating.
- Money often leads to greed. Most of the dysfunctions in our national economy can be traced to the greed of large institutions as well as individual behaviors. "Man never has what he wants," wrote C. F. Ramuz (1878–1947), "because what he wants is everything."
- The recent Great Recession revealed huge holes in our economic system that have been very difficult to correct.
- Recessions are recurrent and painful. As soon as we escape a recession, people begin repeating the same pattern of risky behaviors.
- Money contributes to the pathologies of prosperity, especially obesity and diabetes.
- Money often stratifies us in biblically unacceptable ways.

- People are increasingly drawn into money-making careers rather than people-serving careers.
- Money issues are a leading cause of divorce.
- Money is earned by working, allowing us to buy possessions. But money, working, and possessions cannot buy community, faith, or family, nor relief from loneliness, anxiety, or depression.
- Money has disreputable friends and feeds unsavory passions. It has been said that pornography paid for much of the development of the Internet.
- People are worshipped atop their spectacular wealth but never challenged. Bill Gates and Warren Buffett each sat on $50 *billion* of personal wealth. How does money warrant an ethics exemption of this magnitude? They later began to fund foundations although without personal sacrifice. I do not wish to sound mean-spirited, but I honestly find such behavior incomprehensible. "If anyone has the world's goods and sees his brother in need, yet closes his heart against him, how does God's love abide in him?"[12]

UP, UP, AND AWAY

You can easily detect my concern over the rapid ascendance of the power of money in today's world. To be sure, money has always had power, and from the very outset, even in the Torah, the Scriptures warned against this danger. If this uneasiness was true several millennia ago, what must be said about our modern relationship with money?

Since Adam Smith published *Wealth of Nations* in 1776 (interesting date), money entered the scene more a savior than a demon. The newly systematized science of economics went right to work on behalf of the entire world, helping coordinate the Industrial Revolution and lifting a significant percentage of the world's population out of destitution. Of course there was corruption and greed as always—just read Dickens— but the overall positive effect was not only unprecedented but almost miraculous.

Actually, it was progress leading the charge, not economics. Since the beginning of the Industrial Revolution, progress was the teacher in this classroom and economics its pupil. Combined, they were marvelous to behold and began producing results never before imagined. The thousands of advantages surrounding us today are the direct result of progress working in tandem with economics.

At some point in the past thirty or forty years, however, progress switched from servant to master. It happened so quickly most did not notice. God did. It was so natural an occurrence that most did not care. God did. Progress today runs the West and increasingly the entire world. Its modus operandi is to give us *more and more of everything faster and faster*, a process most people do not understand. God does.

One morning the world woke up to find that the process of progress was now irreversible. Why? Because this process—more and more of everything faster and faster—feeds the world economy, and without progress to feed it, the world economy would starve to death. In other words, if progress were to stop, the economy would crash and never recover.

Do I want progress to stop? Not particularly. Progress is a gift from God and a biblically normative idea that has done remarkable good.

Do I mind if the world economy crashes? Of course I do. That would hurt billions of people, start devastating wars, and consign untold millions to starvation.

Do I therefore want the twin engines of progress and the economy to continue growing their dominating power at this rate? That is precisely the question we must be asking. No, I certainly do not. Apart from God, nothing should be allowed such power in our lives, or, quite frankly, in our world. This unbridled process of power and dominance, accelerating at exponential rates, will inevitably lead to dysfunction and destruction.

If progress and economics are not undergirded by righteousness, ethics, integrity, honesty, and, yes, even a touch of humility, they will tumble into disaster. The erupting of such predictable dysfunctions has already been evident for years.

Education—The educational system is in financial trouble from kindergarten to grad school. Public education costs have soared, quality has not, and troubled state budgets do not have the funds for the nationwide per year per student cost of $10,600.[13] Universities have raised fees five times as fast as inflation over the past thirty years,[14] and a crisis in higher education is inevitable. Students now owe a trillion dollars on college loans, but many cannot find employment.

Health Care—The health-care system has been fiscally dysfunctional for over two decades. Our current costs are eighteen percent of our economy. I recently saw a forty-thousand-dollar ICU bed. One hospital's operating room charges eighty-eight dollars *a minute*. Medicare is rapidly running out of money. Medicaid is an enormous state budget burden. Doctors graduating from medical school owe an average of $155,000, and some over $400,000. I hold all parties in this system responsible: hospitals, pharmaceutical companies, insurance companies, malpractice attorneys, physicians, patients, and the government.

Politics—The political system now spends $2 billion for presidential elections, the senate goes years without producing a budget, and the approval of Congress is at 12 percent. The Federal debt is increasing $3 billion every day. The U.S. government borrows forty cents of every dollar it spends, writes over eighty million checks per month, has recently been running trillion-dollar annual deficits (previous high $450 billion), and owes $1–2 trillion to China. "We hate you guys," said one Chinese Treasury official, "but we can't stop doing this." An International Monetary Fund director wrote, "If you make a list of the countries in the world that have the biggest homework in restoring their public finances to a reasonable situation in terms of debt levels, you find four countries: Greece, Ireland, Japan and the United States."[15] Interesting company. Greek and Irish bonds are junk rated, while Japan has been in economic doldrums for two decades.

Economy—As I write this, the U.S. is still mired in the backwash of The Great Recession. Former Treasury Secretary Larry Summers said we are "now half way to a lost economic decade."[16] *Summa cum lousy* as one commentator called it. It started when the economic system "fell off a cliff," and we were "hours away from the collapse of our economy." Lehman Brothers announced bankruptcy in September 2008, triggering an emergency bailout proposal because, "If we don't do this, we may not have an economy on Monday." Unemployment and housing fell into a deep hole and got stuck there. From when the housing bubble burst in 2006 until mid-2012, home prices nationwide fell 32 percent—even though Alan Greenspan said such things never happen. Of all the homes currently holding mortgages, a staggering 70.5 percent of the total home value is debt.[17] The middle class is shriveled. Goldman Sachs said they had seen "25-standard-deviation moves several days in a row," essentially something that would not even happen once in one hundred millennia.[18] According to the 2009 Davos World Economic Forum, 40 percent of the world's wealth was destroyed in the previous five quarters. On May 6, 2010, the Dow dropped precipitously 999 points in thirty minutes, losing $800 billion. Then in the next twenty minutes, $600 billion came back. No one had the slightest idea what was happening. The Bowles-Simpson Debt Commission report concluded: "If the U.S. does not put its house in order, the reckoning will be sure and the devastation severe." The report was submitted and promptly shelved.

Something different is happening here. It remains to be seen if we will emerge out of this painful time and revert to some normalcy in our economic patterns or whether we will need to adapt to a new economic reality. It must also be said that the origin of this entire mess came from unforgivable greed, incomprehensibly sloppy regulatory oversight, the utter foolishness of a recurrent belief that bubbles will continue even though they never do, and the moral recklessness of high finance making long-shot bets knowing they will get rich if they win and be bailed out with public money if they lose.

If we insist on having gold as our god, we deserve the consequences of that choice. "Some people, eager for money, have wandered from the faith and pierced themselves with many griefs."[19]

ESCAPING ENTRAPMENT

Our economy is 70 percent driven by consumer demand, retail spending, and consumptive activity. What happens, though, when we already have too much stuff, don't need any more, and don't have money to pay for it anyway? It is hard to imagine how an economy so heavily structured on consumption can be sustained. Or, for that matter, whether it is healthy.

Here are some prescriptions that might help us gain control of the money issues in our lives and submit them to the control of the kingdom. While individuals can do little to change our economic system, there is much we can do to prevent from being trapped by it. It is no surprise that contentment wishes to play a part in this rescue.

Rx: 1   *Base Contentment on God Rather Than Economics*

God promised He would never leave us or forsake us. Money cannot give such a promise. Proverbs says, "Trust in the LORD with all your heart."[20] Proverbs also says, "Those who trust in their riches will fall."[21] The Bible says that loving God is the highest of all commandments. It also says that loving money leads to destruction. Why, then, do we continue to believe that money is the secret to contentment?

The road to a contented life is to love God and to use money. Inverting the two is like brushing our teeth with arsenic.

Rx: 2   *Stop Thinking Primarily in Money Terms*

I have met people who seem to have cash registers for brains. When they blink, you can see dollar signs tattooed on their eyelids. Money is always on their minds. It is wise to be informed about personal finances, and, in an environment like this, it is good to be vigilant and cautious. But the Bible reminds us we should put our minds and affections on things above, not on things of this earth:

> Do not love the world or anything in the world. If anyone loves the world, love for the Father is not in them. For everything in the world—the lust of the flesh, the lust of the eyes, and the pride of life—comes not from the Father but from the world. The world

and its desires pass away, but whoever does the will of God lives forever.[22]

This does not mean we are never to think about money but only that we are to think about money in the proper way. It is a tool. An important tool. A tool that can do much good. A tool that also can cause much harm.

With this in mind, the Bible would say we are free to think about money but only after we have thought first about God. Money is our servant, not our master. It is not even our friend. It is only a tool.

Rx: 3   *Pursue Activities That Don't Cost Money*

Does joy cost money? Of course not. That is a silly notion. Our modern version of joy costs money, but that is only the experience of an extremely tiny slice of humanity throughout history. People have been finding sources of joy for centuries without spending a penny.

If God is our source of joy, it is ludicrous to attach a price tag. The Bible speaks hundreds of times about joy, and the context is never related to finances. Paul, in prison, wrote the Epistle of Joy to the people of Philippi and, for good measure, threw in his transcendent teachings about contentment — all while in chains.

How then, in practical terms, does this work? Joy, contentment, and happiness are gifts God gives us through our friends. First of all, Jesus, our infinite friend, and then the community of family and friends around us. This is what we see when visiting impoverished countries known for their joy. They are laughing with neighbors, talking at the bazaar, and visiting along the way and in churches. They are not shy. Laughter is the norm, and it is heard in all settings. The West, where we have replaced biblical joy with financial joy, has become poor in friendship joy.

There are as many joy opportunities as there are creative imaginations. Reading a good book can offer a literary journey around the world or across the ages. Try going for a walk, tending flowers, sitting by rivers, attending free concerts in the park, watching people (especially kids), arriving early for parades, digging a few worms in the yard and tossing a bobber in the lake. Gas is expensive, so switch to bikes. Linda finds great joy in baking breads and delivers them all over the city. With a little practice and creativity, this is easy.

Activities that do not require money, especially community, friend-ship, and hospitality, nevertheless constitute a rich lifestyle. Currently the script for our lives is individualistic and dominated by media, tech-nology, and money. But if we moved from a consumptive to a more communitarian lifestyle, we would quickly discover the benefits in our contentment level.

Part of this picture is the rediscovery of how to savor experiences, events, and food. The speed and intensity of our day have deprived us of this ability to savor. We seldom allow anything to linger long enough to truly appreciate it. Savoring as a lifestyle, *by itself*, has the ability to restore a measure of joy and contentment.

Rx: 4   *Explore Employment Options*

It is perfectly acceptable to look for a better job, for work that is more satisfying and has better pay. For some people, this is precisely what is needed to have more contentment. God is not sadistic and He doesn't want us suffering day after day about an endless pile of delinquent bills. But if He does not grant a betterment in our conditions, then our spiritual responsibility is to be content to "live within our harvest."

It is also reasonable to reassess this issue on a regular basis. Just because God did not throw open doors last year does not mean He's locked them forever. Perhaps He wishes us to look in other directions, to change careers, to go back to school, to move to a different location, or simply to learn valuable lessons about waiting. If we have done all there is to do, and God grants no increase, then we reach for the strength to be content, at least for this season. Perhaps even thanking Him for any opportunity to learn discipline.

Finally, if we sense God's strong calling to a specific path, then we should work our calling and let God provide. Expect Him to make a way. "Next to faith this is the highest art," said Martin Luther (1483–1546), "to be content with the calling in which God has placed you."

Rx: 5   *Do Not Take Orders from Money*

People have a tendency to bow to money. They recognize its power and decide they will do anything to serve it. They worship it. They love it. They live for it. They die for it. They kill for it. They take their instructions from it. They listen to its priests. They study its bible. They talk about it incessantly. They list it as their highest priority. They come together in large meetings to discover how to be better disciples. They weep when it is taken away. They spend so much time serving its purposes that they neglect their own health, relationships, and sleep.

This behavior is not for the people of God. We should resist the *force* of money whenever we feel it. It is powerful, but it is not God. Obviously, this does not mean we stop using money. But when it tells us what to think, how to act, whom to befriend, whom to defriend, and what our priorities are, then it is time to remind money it is for God alone to make such determinations.

Rx: 6   *Don't Link Self-Esteem to Money*

God judges us by what He sees inside, and He never makes mistakes. He does not walk through our houses to see if we are trendy enough to qualify for His favor. He does not examine our transcript in school to see if we made the appropriate grades. He does not hack into our bank account to see if it is respectable. He does not examine our social calendar to see if we have the right friends.

Sometimes it requires a righteous ego strength to go against the flow of our culture. Then, however, we remember Jesus walked opposite the prevailing winds years ago and told us to follow His example. If we are fully surrendered to Christ's sacrifice, then nothing else matters. "The only thing I have to be ashamed of," said Tozer, "is sin."

We are what God knows us to be. Let that be enough.

Rx: 7   *Go Ahead, Buy the New Sofa, Maybe*

If the couch is geriatric, we are not necessarily required to be content with it. If we have the funds and feel God smile, buy a newer one. But if we repeatedly are wanting another couch, a different couch, a new couch, a more fashionable couch, a couch like the neighbors', a couch that makes us feel good about ourselves, then I doubt God is still smiling.

Remember, it is fine to buy a new couch, as long as we remember it is not about the couch. Just as it is not about the clothes, curtains, computer, car, carpet, camera, or cabin.

Rx: 8 Resist Saying, "I Will Be Content When . . ."

Contentment in God, His provision, presence, and providence, is not a postponable commodity. There is no contentment deferral clause in the Bible that says, "exempt if ___."

I do not mean to sound insensitive. If someone is suffering grievously, my heart breaks to hear it. By all means, I will join that person in petitioning God to allow a generous increase in supply. Still, it is a mistake to draw a line and say we will be content only when . . .

The Bible does not say *be content when you have*; it says *be content with what you have*. True contentment is based not on contingencies but on God alone.

MIXING CURRENCIES

Love is the currency of the spiritual world. *Money* is the currency of the material world. God does not want us to *love money*. This is mixing currencies, and it is dangerous. God can easily see if we love the world above or the world below by measuring our regard for spiritual love versus earthly money. This single measurement will tell Him all He needs to know.

Years ago, Dr. Al Weir was a missionary doctor in Nigeria. One afternoon he was walking through a village with the pastor. They entered the concrete-block, dirt-floor home of an elderly Christian woman who was nearly blind. "When the pastor introduced us, she bobbed her head with a grin of pure joy. After she was assured that I was seated, she took a small plate, dusted it off, reached up under the tablecloth and pulled out a small coin. The coin was a kobo, worth less than the widow's mite but valuable to her. She placed the kobo on the plate and held it out to me as a gift for my visit."

Can you imagine being presented with a penny from an elderly, nearly blind African woman who had nothing? "And yet, in that dirt floor room with poverty and personal tragedies that I can only imagine, she stands there in my memory, holding out that kobo as a precious gift to me out of love."[23]

She was not giving money; she was giving love. Joyfully. This is a different kind of wealth, and it belongs to the same family as "godliness with contentment is great gain."

CHAPTER 10

CONTENTMENT AND SUFFERING

The Indispensable Gift

God had one son on earth without sin, but never one without suffering.

— St. Augustine

Elaine Eng, a graduate of Princeton University and Albert Einstein College of Medicine, was in the middle of her OB/GYN residency. Every specialty training program is a challenge, but at least with obstetrics you have the wondrous privilege of seeing babies born. Dr. Eng, however, had two problems: She wasn't "seeing" anything well, and she had babies of her own at home.

She made an appointment to consult an ophthalmologist about her sight. It didn't take long to diagnose the problem: retinitis pigmentosa. She was going blind. Tears, anguish, hysteria? A Christian for eight years, Dr. Eng first thing thanked the Lord. Then she resigned her residency program and went home.

"The Lord had already started working in my heart to somehow begin to cope with this diagnosis before I'd even heard of it," Dr. Eng said. "I was in a residency with two children: a baby and a toddler. I was torn between my children and my job. When I heard the news, I was startled but then blessed to realize that this was part of the Lord's answer to my dilemma. There was no point in continuing in a surgical subspecialty. That would not be ethical. I resigned that day, thanked the Lord, went home, and had some of the greatest years being a full-time mother.

"This so-called 'tragedy' in my life was very much for the good. I had the chance to 'see' and care for my children during those precious young years. To play with them, sing songs, teach them, feed them, and do all those wonderful mothering things that many take for granted. And now that they are grown, I can see in my mind's eye all those great images and memories. I enjoyed motherhood so much that I would not have changed my life in any way if given the chance."

After her blindness was complete and her children a bit older, she returned to medicine and switched to psychiatry. Psychiatrists know all the stages of grief, but Dr. Eng says her personal experience was different from the textbooks. "At the moment of diagnosis and the four years following, I did not experience any of that and I have to say that is not normal, but it is Christian and divine. This is the only way, as a psychiatrist, I can explain it. The initial diagnosis was received by me as a good thing, and it did work out well in so many ways."

Who talks like this but a person sent contentment from another world?

Twenty years later, this distinguished fellow of the American Psychiatric Association and graduate of prestigious universities is still thanking the ophthalmologist for telling her the diagnosis in such a gentle manner. In addition, she has just increased her involvement with the Alliance Theological Seminary Graduate School of Counseling in New York City to full-time faculty.[1]

UNIVERSAL AND UNAVOIDABLE

Suffering is an unavoidable part of life. Everyone's life, no exceptions. We don't much like this fact and desperately wish there were a way around it, but there isn't.

Progress does not release us from the unavoidability of suffering. Neither does being a "success" or even being a Christian. Education does not stop suffering from happening, nor does science, technology, transportation, labor-saving devices, or affluence. Suffering is universal across the globe and across history.

It is a surprise to many, even a shock, that progress, success, and being a Christian do not prevent suffering. To clarify, these factors do indeed solve many specific types of suffering. Thanks to progress, for example, polio is very rare today, and we are glad to be done with it. As for being a Christian, that of course solves the biggest problem we will ever have. Nevertheless, there are tens of thousands of ways in which we suffer, and they are all floating in the unending stream of life. Search as we might, we will never find a section of the river that is pain free.

The past had its forms of suffering; the present has its forms of suffering; the future will have its forms of suffering. In some respects these are different, and in many respects these are the same. Suffering manifests itself in various ways—physical, emotional, relational, spiritual, financial—all a part of the human condition.

A LIFE WITHOUT SUFFERING?

If we could choose a life without suffering, would we? Most would answer quickly: *of course*. To be done with headaches, literal and figurative. No overdue bills, flat tires, broken relationships, cancer, disunity in the church, political fighting, low back pain, insomnia, or hurricanes. An end to stress, overload, anger, frustration, depression, anxiety, and panic. Technology would always function perfectly, my computer would never freeze, and the Cubs would always win.

As tempting as this sounds, we would do well to consider a deeper thought: *A life without suffering is a one-way ticket to superficial Christianity.* There are some lessons in life, often the most important ones, that can be learned only through the gift of pain.

Consider literature. If suffering disappeared from the world, nearly all great fiction would disappear as well. Gone are the works of Dickens,

Melville, half of Shakespeare, and all of the Russians. There go *Lord of the Rings*, *Pilgrim's Progress*, and *Les Misérables* as well.

GOD'S ROLE IN SUFFERING

How about the Bible? That, too, would disappear, for the Bible is full of suffering from beginning to end. The message, however, is not about hopelessness and despair. On the contrary, we are now on holy ground discussing a secret that involves God, contentment, authenticity, and freedom. If the Bible is full of suffering, it is also full of redemption. For the Christian, these two always go together.

God is very aware of the problem of suffering. He understands it completely, is aware when it is happening to us, and has a suffering agenda for each of our lives.

When we wake up tomorrow, God will be at our side. He has a toolbox, and each day He chooses the tools that fit our situation best. Sometimes that includes suffering. He looks at us, looks at suffering, and decides this is the very best tool for our lives, the only tool that can accomplish what is needed.

The Christian life is a series of deeper deaths. If we wish to continue on a deepening path with Christ, then suffering is an ideal instrument in the Lord's hand to accomplish this. A life without suffering would yield an inferior spiritual product.

Suffering seen in this way becomes a gift. It is the kind of gift we do not particularly want, but, still, the kind of gift that is essential if we wish to be fully conformed to Christ. This is where contentment comes in. We embrace suffering with less resistance when we sense the hand of God. We learn to say with Paul, "We also glory in our sufferings, because we know that suffering produces perseverance; perseverance, character; and character, hope. And hope does not put us to shame, because God's love has been poured out into our hearts through the Holy Spirit, who has been given to us."[2] Only God starts with suffering and ends with hope and love.

Do we want to be perfected in the faith? Then we must allow God to use suffering to accomplish this purpose. Do we want to deepen our character? Do we want to be mature? Patient? More sensitive and compassionate? Do we want more perseverance and patience in our spiritual lives? Nothing builds these qualities like suffering.

God has a role in our suffering because He is always about the task of transformation. Christlikeness is the goal, and there is not a moment in which God is not active on behalf of our spiritual betterment.

It is not that God enjoys seeing us suffer but rather that He enjoys seeing us deepen. God is not sadistic. In fact, Scripture is very clear that God is compassionate toward us.[3] Not only is He compassionate toward us and present with us during our suffering, but theologian John Stott maintains that God actually suffers with us. "There is good biblical evidence that God not only suffered in Christ, but that God in Christ suffers with his people still. . . . It is wonderful that we may share in Christ's sufferings; it is more wonderful still that he shares in ours."[4]

After the experience of suffering, we are different than we were before. If we allow God to use the experience for His purposes, we will not only be different, we will also be better.

A DANGEROUS COLLISION OF POWER

Suffering is often a powerful experience and therefore entails risk. Whenever power of any kind shows up in our vicinity, it is important for us to measure its intentions. We should never make the mistake of yawning through power encounters.

For God's part, He wants to use the power of suffering to mold, teach, deepen, purify, and refine us. Yes, and even to strengthen us. It is comforting to know that the greatest Power in the universe is for us and not against us.

Satan, however, is also powerful and has a very different agenda. We are not well-acquainted with the Evil One and feel more comfortable if we can keep him in a semi-fantasy state. His work, therefore, is under-estimated. Make no mistake: He will ruin us in any way possible. We should therefore remain on guard. "Be self-controlled and alert," wrote Peter. "Your enemy the devil prowls around like a roaring lion looking for someone to devour. Resist him, standing firm in the faith, because you know that the family of believers throughout the world is undergoing the same kind of sufferings."[5]

Satan wants to use the power of suffering to destroy us, and he often succeeds. Some leave the faith, some leave their families, some forsake life itself. This is why God does not leave us alone during such times — even when it feels as if He does. If we are believers who put our trust in His Word, God will never allow us to be tempted to despair beyond what we are able to bear.[6]

THE PASSION OF THE CHRIST

A critical part of our suffering story is the example of Jesus Himself. To be frank, I have always wondered why Jesus needed to suffer so severely. Blood was required, and so was death. This I understand. The atonement demands it, the Old Testament prescribes it, and without the shedding of blood and dying there is no remission of sin. But why, exactly, was it necessary for Him to suffer as He did? Could not redemption perhaps have been accomplished by Christ going straight to the cross, being roped there instead of nailed, and then speared in the side ten minutes later by impatient centurions?

This, however, was not the Father's plan. His will required more, and it is a realization that should challenge me the next time I complain about stale bread. The Messiah's suffering was eloquently foretold in Isaiah 53 and then explained in advance by Jesus Himself.[7] I yield to the Father, thank Christ for His willingness, and ponder what this means for my own willingness.

Hebrews 2 goes on to explain it was fitting that the Author of salvation be made complete, or perfect, through suffering.[8] In addition, Jesus suffered in order that He would be able to help those who are tempted.[9] Not that Jesus ever lacked anything, but only in the sense that somehow the man Jesus was ordained to experience human suffering at a particularly deep level in order for His redemptive purposes to be complete.

How sobering to realize Jesus did this readily. How unsettling to my own sources of discontent to watch this bleeding Messiah suffer in my place without protest.

It is one thing to be content with an older automobile or empty piggy bank. But contentment with a cross? With the suffering of a crucifixion?

THE FELLOWSHIP OF HIS SUFFERINGS

Because of the finished work of Christ, we have become reconciled to God. We are grafted in, completely accepted, and joint heirs. But God loves us too much to exempt us from the privileges of our adoption. With royalty comes high honors and responsibilities, all a part of our new journey to become like Christ. And, to our joy, it includes sharing His sufferings.

Listen to Paul, who always seems to run toward suffering rather than away. "Now if we are children, then we are heirs — heirs of God and co-heirs with Christ, if indeed we share in his sufferings in order that we may also share in his glory."[10] This is not just contentment to suffer, but an enthusiastic willingness to climb up on the cross next to Christ. "I want to know Christ — yes to know the power of his resurrection and participation in his sufferings, becoming like him in his death."[11] How can any of us claim this verse without a special dispensation of contentment for the most difficult, yet perhaps most glorious, experience in any Christian life?

Peter, too, is caught up in the same theme. "Therefore, since Christ suffered in his body, arm yourselves also with the same attitude, because whoever suffers in the body is done with sin."[12] You can sense that Peter does not speak about a guilt-ridden obligation but instead an authentic kind of joy and contentment. "Dear friends, do not be surprised at the fiery ordeal that has come on you to test you, as though something strange were happening to you. But rejoice inasmuch as you participate in the sufferings of Christ, so that you may be overjoyed when his glory is revealed."[13]

We come to understand that suffering is an integral part of the normal Christian life. Instead of an enemy, it is an ally. If it would depart from us, we would risk losing touch with both depth and transcendence. Suffering makes us strong and gives us roots. Unless I miss my guess, the church will need to reacquire this type of fortitude in the challenging days ahead.

Paul further rounds out his perspective on suffering in his second letter to the Corinthians. "For the sake of Christ, then, I am content with weaknesses, insults, hardships, persecutions, and calamities. For when I am weak, then I am strong."[14] Content? This is the authentic testimony of a person who never turned from the way of Christ. His words to the elders at Ephesus as recorded in Acts, give an even broader perspective. The occasion is their final good-bye, accompanied by much grieving, weeping, and embracing. Although we have seen this verse in an earlier chapter, listen to Paul again in this context: "I consider my life worth nothing to me, my only aim is to finish the race and complete the task the Lord Jesus has given me — the task of testifying to the good news of God's grace."[15] For me, it is one of the most compelling verses in the Bible.

TOO VALUABLE TO WASTE

Forgive me if I have appeared too naïve about the extraordinary pain of suffering. The last thing I wish to do is wound the already wounded. Be assured — I am well experienced with pain. Yet as acquainted as I am with suffering on many fronts, my higher allegiance is always given to God's view on these matters. It is abundantly clear that He has traveled a great distance to join us in our battle, all in the name of the boldest rescue mission ever conceived. Nothing will stand in the way of His final victory over this ghastly foe, and perhaps that end is already in sight. Our role, as we wait, is cooperation and contentment.

Knowing that every person reading this book has experienced suffering, I offer some prescriptions that might help us understand the secret power gained from hearing what God would say to His people.

Rx: 1   *Share the Suffering*

The wolves wait until the sick, lame, elderly, or young fall back from the herd, then they move in for the kill. Similarly, enemy submarines wait until a ship falls back from its convoy. Then they fire their torpedoes and run for safety. My father, who served as a signalman in the U.S. Navy during WWII, called it coffin corner. He said it was not a pleasant place to be.

People are often isolated by suffering. They are anxious, depressed, and lonely. In the midst of the pain, they don't know what to say or how to say it. They fall back from the herd; they lose the protection of the convoy. Friends and acquaintances sense an awkwardness and shy away. This isolation compounds the pain, often severely so.

That is why, within the church, we have a biblically mandated requirement to help one another endure suffering, to protect those who are vulnerable and at risk. "Carry each other's burdens, and in this way you will fulfill the law of Christ,"[16] is not only a commandment but a privilege.

Just as we share in the sufferings of Christ, so we share in the sufferings of each other. I have frequently prayed that God would transfer some of another person's pain onto me, a literal "carrying" of another's burden. Romans 12:15 tells us to "mourn with those who mourn." For us to weep with those whose life is weeping joins us together in a mystical way. This not only has the feeling of being healthy, it is proven to be healthy.

A Danish proverb says that shared sorrow is half a sorrow. Sharing in this way decreases our pain and increases our endurance. The presence of godly others reminds us of the presence of God.

Rx: 2   *Thank God*

Praise is a powerful painkiller, and so is gratitude. Some think it impossible, if not insane, to invoke these responses in the midst of suffering, but that is not the opinion of Scripture. James tells us to "Consider it all joy, my bretheren, when you encounter various trials, knowing that the testing of your faith produces endurance. And let endurance have [its] perfect result, so that you may be perfect and complete, lacking in nothing."[17]

Perseverance, it seems, is a popular theme in this context as we already saw Paul reminding us to "glory in our sufferings" because it produces perseverance, character, hope, and love.[18] Peter, too, tells us to "rejoice inasmuch as you participate in the sufferings of Christ."[19] In Acts 5:41, the apostles were flogged, then went away "rejoicing because they had been counted worthy of suffering disgrace for the Name."

This seems like an unusual strategy for confronting pain, but then so is contentment. Such responses are counterintuitive and countercultural. They also have the surprising advantage of being effective. It is not just that the Bible tells us to be grateful, joyous, and content, although that would be reason enough. But it is also the surprising realization that God, by making such responses available to us in the midst of our discomfort, is showing His compassion.

A response of thanksgiving, praise, and contentment depends partly on our personality, partly on the severity of the suffering, and partly on our spiritual maturity. In my own case, for whatever the reason, I feel closer to God when I am suffering than at any other time. This intimacy is so precious that I yearn for it when it is absent. No, I am not a masochist, and I never seek pain. But when it comes, I know I will be held by Christ throughout the duration.

We thank God because He is in the process of being good to us even when it doesn't feel like that is true. We thank Him because when it seems as if He is tearing us down, He is actually building us up. We thank Him because at the end of this painful season, we will be stronger, deeper, and more perfectly conformed to Christ.

Rx: 3   *Complain to God*

It may seem strange to jump from thanking to complaining, but we cannot keep secrets from God. He knows better than we do what our thoughts and feelings are. It is not wrong to complain *to* God as long as we do not complain *about* God.

There are as many psalms that complain to God as praise Him. Take David, for example, in Psalm 13:1-4:

How long, LORD? Will you forget me forever?
How long will you hide your face from me?
How long must I wrestle with my thoughts
and day after day have sorrow in my heart?
How long will my enemy triumph over me?

Look on me and answer, LORD my God.
Give light to my eyes, or I will sleep in death,
and my enemy will say, "I have overcome him,"
and my foes will rejoice when I fall.

If we are disappointed and our heart is discouraged, it is okay to say, "How long, O Lord, how long?" But it is never okay to accuse God or try to hide from Him. Such emotional reactions will only disrupt our closeness and double our suffering.

David was so intimate with God that he knew it was futile trying to hide his feelings. He also knew his love for God was exceeded only by God's love for him. They were friends, and an honest discussion did not threaten that relationship. After his complaint in the first four verses, he completely changes direction in the final two, "But I trust in your unfailing love; my heart rejoices in your salvation. I will sing to the LORD, for he has been good to me." Not a hint of pretense, just a deep disappointment wrapped in a deeper contentment.

Rx: 4   *Never Waste the Pain*

One of the greatest tragedies I see in life is when people go through enormous levels of suffering but come out on the other side having learned nothing. This is hard for me to witness because I know such a response will only prolong the suffering and deprive this person of the kind of growth God has in mind. Why does God allow suffering in the first place? To make us better people.

In some ways, this entire discussion is similar to athletics. Without suffering in sports, there is no improvement, no development, no strengthening. We sign up because we wish to have fun and participate in an interesting activity but also so we can increase our abilities and endurance. We work out, do some running, lift some weights, improve our conditioning, practice-practice-practice, all of which makes our muscles hurt and body sweat — and it feels great.

The same is true in the military. Boot camp is gruesome, but at the end, a person feels proud to have endured.

Suffering, of course, is not voluntary like athletics and military service. And suffering involves different tactics. But in the end, it aims for a similar result. Our body hurts, our brain hurts, our spirit hurts, we cry, we can't sleep, we endure high levels of stress and anguish, we cry some more, we wonder if we can possibly make it around the next lap. But when the dark night clears and we graduate to what comes next, we have gained perseverance, character, patience, strength, experience, sensitivity, compassion, maturity, depth, and fortitude. Granted, it is a risky strategy, but there is no other way God can give us such accelerated growth.

Remember always that this loving God suffered for us and suffers with us still. It is safe to trust Him in the storm, to have contentment in His will, and to wait for understanding until later.

Rx: 5   *Welcome the Lesson*

It has been said that adversity introduces a person to himself. No one fully knows their capacities until they have been challenged. How much suffering can we bear? How deep can we go? How strong can we be? Einstein's life was an unmitigated disaster for his first twenty-five years until one day "a storm broke loose in my mind." He had finally tapped into "God's thoughts," and the rest is history. He went on to earn the Nobel Prize and be named the Person of the Century.

I am often saddened by the general lack of fortitude in our country and churches. In Solzhenitsyn's 1978 commencement address to Harvard University, he began,

> A decline in courage may be the most striking feature that an outside observer notices in the West today. The Western world has lost its civic courage, both as a whole and separately, in each country, in each

government, in each political party. Such a decline in courage is particularly noticeable among the ruling and intellectual elites, causing an impression of a loss of courage by the entire society.[20]

Others have suggested I not be so hasty. When an extreme challenge comes into a life or into a nation, it is surprising how many of us suddenly find strength we never knew existed. September 11th was such an event. I was very proud of our conduct during those weeks.

Suffering is a rigorous classroom. Will we embrace the lessons learned? Will we put in the effort to pass all the tests? A crown awaits those who succeed. Francis Frangipane wrote,

> Life consists of learning lessons and passing tests. The integrity of God requires that our learning not be mere head knowledge but that our hearts be conformed to Christ. Indeed, before the Lord is through with us, the way of Christ will be more than something we know; it will be something we instinctively choose in the midst of temptation or battle. This is where we graduate into the power of God.[21]

GOD IS

In 1931, converts to Christianity in the Congo began sensing the call to become missionaries themselves. Because of tribal animosities, it was a dangerous notion, yet godly as well. One "insignificant" man named Zamu felt moved to evangelize a traditional enemy tribe, but he had "a large ulcerous wound on his leg which would not heal and which compelled him to walk on the toes of one foot."

One day he came and told the missionary lady about this vision. She doubted his ability to survive and felt compelled to test his call.

"What about your foot, Zamu?"

"God is, White Lady."

"But the food is so different down there; no palm oil, no salt down there."

"But God is, White Lady."

"You might starve or be killed."

"God is, White Lady."

"What about your wife?"

"She will accompany me. God is, White Lady."

Zamu indeed succeeded in making the long trip and established a ministry. Not only that, but he also succeeded in inspiring many of his tribe to travel in all directions telling of the Good News. Zamu sorely missed salt in his diet, and finally, after a year, prayed to God about it. Two weeks later, a large packet of salt arrived—from the White Lady.[22]

CHAPTER 11

CONTENTMENT AND AUTHENTICITY

What Jesus Knows Us to Be

We are all so conditioned by the world in which we live that we can go a lifetime and never get within a stone's throw of our own true selves.

— Bob Benson

Rich Williams is a strong man — in several ways. A decade ago, this six foot three, 330-pound, All-American defensive lineman was projected to be a mid-round selection in the NFL draft. He had one visit with the Miami Dolphins but then told his agent to cancel his other trips. He was dropping out.

The sporting world was thunderstruck. What? Are you crazy? You don't want to be famous and earn millions playing pro football? Why don't you at least go through the draft and collect your six-figure signing bonus? You don't have to continue after that if you don't feel like it.

"That would have been like stealing, almost like robbing a bank, and there's no honor in that," he told *USA Today*. "I try to be a good Christian man, and I don't want to cheat a team that believes in me. Not only that, but how would I feel taking a draft spot from some other guy that had worked his whole life just to get to that point."

It turns out he had been falling out of love with the game of football for a while, but because of his size and performance, he still drew lots of media attention. "I came here to get a degree, not [play in] the NFL, and you can only hide how you feel for so long.

"Money doesn't make me happy and, to me, money isn't the true meaning of success. It's family. It's people who love you. It's being true to yourself. If you're not true to yourself, how can you be true to anything?"

He went on to become one of the strongest men in America—if not the strongest.[1] It takes strength to lift those weights. It takes perhaps even more strength to pass up wads of "free" money.

Ten years later, here comes another. Left-handed pitcher Gil Meche told the Kansas City Royals they could keep the $12.4 million owed him. Meche came over from the Mariners in 2007 and signed a five-year megacontract. He was voted an All-Star that season and pitched well for a couple years. Then injuries set in, and his pitching shoulder simply could not get it done. Early in his final contract year, he told the organization his shoulder was not worth the money they were required to pay him. The Royals should keep it.

You're kidding, right? $12.4 *million*?

The decision rocked the baseball world. All he had to do—and what *everyone* else does—is show up for spring training and the money was his. It *belonged* to him, no questions asked. They knew about his shoulder, but a contract is a contract.

A *Sports Illustrated* reporter called his career-ending act "perhaps the most unbelievable finish in Major League baseball history." The Mets manager said, "It's just so odd and rare." A *New York Daily News* reporter said, "By showing our kids what integrity looks like, he's earned *our* respect, too."

"This isn't about being a hero," Meche said. "It just wasn't the right thing to do." He continued, "When I signed my contract, my main goal was to earn it. Once I started to realize I wasn't earning my money, I felt bad. I was making a crazy amount of money for not even pitching. Honestly, I didn't feel like I deserved it. I didn't want to have those feelings again."[2]

CONTENT TO WALK AWAY

Not many injured elites turn down big money these days, especially when agents tell them to grab it and everyone nods in agreement. The power of celebrity sports seems to grant an exemption from common-sense ethics. Not the legalese kind or big-banker-who-got-the-ten-million-bonus-despite-the-scandal kind. I am speaking of the blue-collar neighborhood ethics. The didn't-do-the-job-so-don't-deserve-to-get-paid kind. The we-sleep-better-when-we-do-the-right-thing kind.

When we lay down at night, turn off the lights, and we are all alone — who are we then? In the pitch dark, when we can't even see our hand. Who are we, really?

"Character is what you are in the dark," Dwight L. Moody once said. I might add, authenticity is when we bring character into the light. Authenticity refers to a congruence between our character and our actions.

The story is told of a famous movie star entering a hotel. Two women in the lobby spotted him and ran to intercept him at the elevators.

"Are you the real Robert Redford?"

"Only when I'm alone," he said.

Authentic people sleep better. People who have nothing to hide — from others, from themselves, from God. David said, "Though you probe my heart and examine me at night, though you test me, you will find nothing."[3]

I spent six weeks in 1983 doctoring on the primitive island of Carriacou just north of Grenada. It was just after the U.S. invasion sent all the Cuban physicians scurrying back to Havana. The islanders eat corn and peas from their front yards and fish they catch from boats they build with their own hands. A fisherman invited me to go out one morning, and we climbed into his boat at first light. We made the rounds of his fish pots pulling up exotic species, some beautiful, some frightening.

"Don't touch that one," he'd say. "Poisonous."

At one point, I put my foot in the wrong place and broke through the wooden hull.

"I can fix it," he said with a laugh.

I looked across the bay and saw many other floating markers of different styles and colors. "What keeps you from taking another person's fish?" I asked.

He looked at me and said matter-of-factly, "I want to sleep at night."

This fisherman was content with his catch and did not covet his neighbor's fish. He wanted to walk uprightly in the day and to sleep well in the night. He did not need an ethicist or psychiatrist — or an author — to teach him about being authentic and contented.

There is no way to have biblical authenticity without biblical contentment. They travel together, each making sure we do not compromise the other. If we take money we did not earn, they send us helpful alarms. If we accept undeserved acclaim or assume a higher position than our peers, they launch a shrieking salvo into our conscience. If we start down the road of compromise, they begin with a slap in the face and, if necessary, progress from there. We should thank them, for once we begin to forget who God knows us to be, we enter a confusing moral wasteland. "No man," wrote Hawthorne, "for any considerable period, can wear one face to himself and another to the multitude, without finally getting bewildered as to which may be the true."

FROM SILLINESS TO SACRILEGE

Hypocrite is originally a Greek word related to actors on the stage wearing masks. We all have a degree of pretense within us, and we wear different masks in different situations. Sometimes this is laughable, as when the little boy said, "It all started when Jimmy hit me back." Then the little boy grows into a British rugby coach, like the one who expressed his preference for "getting your retaliations in first."

A few years ago, the secretary general of an African football association ruled that it was okay for officials to take bribes as long as they called an otherwise clean game. "We know match officials are offered money or anything to influence matches and they can accept it," he said. "Referees should only pretend to fall for the bait, but make sure the result doesn't favor those offering the bribe."[4]

What could go wrong in *Bethlehem* at *Christmas* at the *Church of the Nativity?* You'd think being a sweeper in the house of the Lord would be enough for contentment, but the battle happens every year. "About a hundred clergymen from Greek Orthodox and Armenian Apostolic churches, armed with brooms, came to blows during the cleaning of the church in preparation for Orthodox Christmas celebrations," reported Reuters. The recurrent disagreements concern their jurisdictional boundaries. "No one was arrested," said the Palestinian policeman, "because all those involved were men of God."[5]

In Taarbaek, Denmark, a Lutheran pastor said in an interview, "There is no heavenly God, there is no eternal life, there is no resurrection." The shocked Bishop tried to fire him but could not because the government pays the salary. She then insisted he apologize, which leaves the bizarre question about what kind of apology he could possibly make. To complicate matters, the head of the country's Theological College of Education called the pastor's remarks "refreshing."[6]

COMING CLEAN

We snicker and tut-tut at such foolishness and gasp in abhorrence at such clergy behaviors. Then we remember that we, too, fight in churches, and we, too, often live lives and make decisions as if God did not exist.

It is easy, I suppose, to chuckle at the blatant foolishness of others but not as easy to chuckle at that person in the mirror. Yet nothing could be more freeing, and I might add, more urgent, than coming clean with God.

In my mind, spiritual authenticity is the most important test for the church today. We live in a special moment in history, a radical historic discontinuity when the math is not behaving and everything is being shaken. The U.S. has problems, the world system has problems, health care has problems, the economy has problems.

God, on the other hand, has no problems.

What about us? Our families and churches? It depends on authenticity. Only a genuine commitment to God, to His Word, and to our testimony before a watching world has the power to keep us under the shelter of His care. "Blessed are those whose ways are blameless, who walk according to the law of the LORD."[7]

Some think authenticity is a heavy lift. It sounds so introspective and psychoanalytical. Actually, it's not all that hard. Just drop the pretense. Just be who the Bible says we are. Authenticity is simply a matter of agreeing with God about what He knows. "No man is what he himself thinks he is," said Leon Morris. "He is only what Jesus knows him to be."

When we look at it rationally, we might as well be real, because we certainly can't con God. We can play games with others and even with ourselves, and sometimes we get pretty good at it. Some of us have a pretty high capacity to fool ourselves. Be that as it may, none of us can fake it before our Creator. David understood this well. "You perceive my thoughts from afar. . . . You are familiar with all my ways. Before a word is on my tongue you, LORD, know it completely."[8]

We know we have reached full authenticity if, when we die and cross the line, God doesn't have much changing to do. When the difference between our testimony and actual lifestyle is too small to be measured. When our obedience is equal to our knowledge.

If this seems punitive, then you misunderstand my point. It is actually the opposite. Pain and penalty come when we fail to fully yield. The only time guilt drips like acid is when we put on the mask and fake it. But an authentic walk? Once we surrender, once we are fully content to be all in, that is when joy flows like a river. There is no freedom like the kind that comes from a pure heart before the Almighty.

Authenticity is not only about joy and freedom but also about sanctification. It's about kingdom norms rather than cultural norms, about honesty and transparency before God. It's about desiring God and inner purity, about depending on Him and walking in the Spirit. It's about having nothing to hide and being glad to finally be finished with that burden.

The idea is not to try harder. It has little to do with gritting our teeth and forcing righteousness. It is much easier than that. We just give up. We give up our pretense, and, while we are at it, our discontent, worldly desires, revenge, worry, and reputation. That might sound hard, but it really isn't. You just do it. Millions have done it, and it's quite a wonderful feeling.

No one will ever love us as Jesus does. No one will ever know us as He does. Why in the world do we push back against Him? Why do we insist on keeping a portion for ourselves and burying it under the carpet in the floor of the closet? What silliness to think we can hide anything. He made us. He knows our thoughts. He is on a first-name basis with our subatomic particles. He is the lover of our souls. He suffered an infinite hurt when the guilt was infinitely mine. No one will ever be more faithful. What's to hide from? I can't pay Christ back, but one thing I can give Him is an authentic life.

The truth is we will never be happy doing things "my way." We will never be content being what the culture wants us to be. We will only be whole—at peace, at rest, and fully contented—when we agree with God about who we are and about what He wants us to be.

PRECISION AND PURITY

I once had the privilege of going up the St. Louis Arch, and as a Cubs fan, once is probably enough. You ride up in this somewhat scary combination of a train-elevator.

The Arch is 630 feet tall, equal to a sixty-story skyscraper. When they built it, both sides were constructed at the same time. In order for this to succeed, there was need for meticulous precision at every step. First of all, men laying the foundation at the bottom had to do their work without error. Then as the two sides rose up, care had to be taken that they were perfectly symmetrical. If both columns were to connect at the top, there must be no variation. Each night engineers would survey the progress to be sure there was not more than $1/64^{th}$ of an inch variance—the thickness of a fingernail.

I often think of authenticity in these terms. Is it sufficient to shoot for "approximate Christianity" or do we need something more precise? Biblically, exact Christianity is the standard. Not randomness, but all-or-nothing Christianity. If this feels unappealing, like taking out the garbage or going to the dentist, it is really nothing like that at all. It is more like a trip to the Alps. Let's imagine we've been given unlimited access to a high mountain chalet. All we have to do is climb the beautiful slopes, reach the pasture, and occupy the authenticity chalet.

The higher we climb in our spiritual authenticity, the closer we are to God. The view from there is breathtaking, and the other chalets are filled with such wonderful neighbors: joy, peace, contentment, love, grace, kindness, gentleness, and all the rest. Spiritual precision leads to purity of faith, and that makes a very restful home in which to live.

Let me be clear: I am not speaking of perfection. None of us can achieve that, and God does not require it. He has reasonable expectations of us. But if we can't hit *perfection of performance*, we can aim instead for *purity of intention*. This is within our reach. David possessed it. Even when he found himself in repeated trouble and kept saying, "How long?" still he would plead for God to search his intentions and "create in me a pure heart."[9] God does not really need our productivity anyway, but He does mean to have our hearts.

LOVE, CONTENTMENT, AND AUTHENTIC RELATIONSHIPS

If on our deathbeds we were given an opportunity to reroll the video-tape and do one aspect of our lives over, most of us, I am convinced, would pick our relationships—the chance to improve our connections with those we love the most. Indeed, loving relationships are the mandate of eternity, and we neglect them at the peril of not only our happiness but also our testimony.

Love is not the road to authenticity—it *is* authenticity. Love is not just a good idea—it is the only idea. Love is not just the first step—it is the alpha and the omega.

To love is the central commandment of all eternity. To love God, ourselves, and our neighbors should be the first guideline for all life decisions and actions. Until we love, we are not permitted to go further. Without it we are nothing, and we gain nothing.[10] Christ's Great Commandment reduces to one concept: love.[11] Love must precede all else. Secondary emotions may follow, but love is not expected to coexist with other feelings or actions. Instead, all other feelings and actions must coexist with love. If they cannot, they must go. There is no spiritually authentic aspect of living that does not include love.

The family deserves special emphasis here, not only because God ordains it but also because it is one of the great shock absorbers in any society. Yet the shock absorber is itself being shocked. Our troubled families need the foundational blessings of love, contentment, and authenticity to be reaffirmed.

Concerning our marriages, divorce does not begin in the attorney's office but when the first niggling of discontent enters the home. Set your security alarm to detect its presence, then go after it with a spiritual howitzer. Lock the door against it. Sometimes, if you understand my meaning, we have to fight for love. Then turn and bless each other and express gratitude and contentment at every opportunity. Love even when it hurts.

Concerning our children, one of the greatest gifts we can give them is that of biblical contentment. Teach them to be content in a God who knows them, loves them, and will never leave them. This not only has the advantage of being true to Scripture, but practically, it might also afford a measure of peace if the culture bullies them. In many situations, today's youth peer cultures can be difficult to endure. It often seems no youth can measure up unless they are attractive, intelligent, athletic, and rich. Make the home a countercultural place of safety and contentment.

It should also be pointed out that today's youth insist on genuineness. They have good con meters and can easily spot a fraud, particularly if under the same roof. Children will not believe our testimony unless they see us as authentic. All family relationships would benefit if we lived lives of integrity and if we loved each other unconditionally.

PASSING THE TESTS

God does not need to quiz us to find out who we are. We, however, need help assessing our kingdom authenticity. Here are a few such tests.

Leadership, Power—Power often corrupts, as does leadership without servanthood. Abraham Lincoln said, "Nearly all men can stand adversity, but if you want to test a man's character, give him power."

Money, Prosperity, Success—We use the common ploy "I don't love money," and see it work in the court of public opinion. But that court is trumped by the court of God's opinion, and there, our chances are not as good without authenticity. If God blesses us with increase, we do well to remember it is faith that moves mountains, not money or success. A life without prayer is a boast against God.

Service—God knows if our service is for Him to see or for the world to see. If we do it to please the world, we have our reward already. For God's part, He rewards according to authenticity, not according to the deed. Bonhoeffer wrote, "We don't need so much to hide our righteous acts from others as we need to hide them from ourselves."

Giving—Jesus said some announce their generosity "with trumpets." Instead, He preached stealth giving. The Talmud teaches, "He that gives should never remember, he that received should never forget," and also, "Regard it as trifling the great good you did to others, and as enormous the little good others did to you."

Adversity—Adversity is an excellent barometer of authenticity. When the heat is turned up, we all have a point where we show the strain. Do we despair that God has abandoned us, or do we understand God allows adversity to mold us? Perhaps even bow the knee and thank Him for it.

WRENCH OURSELVES LOOSE

It is hard to pray with closed eyes if a thousand buffalo are stampeding twenty feet away. Similarly, Christian disciplines are made more difficult by a culture that is loud, unruly, demanding, pervasive, and increasingly irreverent. Here are some prescriptions that will help keep us on the road to an authentic, contented life.

Rx: 1   *Compare Today with 100 Years from Today*

When we begin the day, what is it we wish to do today? And one hundred years from now, what is it we wish we would have done today? *The latter perspective represents true spiritual authenticity.* From the perspective of eternity, everything will be clarified. What is important will be clearly differentiated from what is unimportant. Gone will be the worries about clothes, cars, or whether the dinner was overcooked. Instead, we will be solely occupied with the kingdom and glory of God. Martin Luther said there were only two days on his calendar: "Today" and "That day." My advice: Today live for That Day. When it comes, we will not be disappointed. "Remember," said Henry van Dyke, "what you possess in the world will be found at the day of your death to belong to someone else, but what you are will be yours forever."

Rx: 2   *Invite Christ to Run Your Life — and Mean It*

How many of us would truly invite Jesus to come into our lives, walk with us for one week, and change anything He wanted? Do we fully understand just how disruptive He would be? Jesus would turn *everything* on its head. Think how this might apply to politicians, doctors, bankers, pastors, football players, mothers, and husbands. Authenticity means allowing Jesus to walk into our lives and mess it up however He wants, and to regard that as a good thing. We not only tolerate it, we invite it. And because it is Jesus, we pledge our contentment with the result.

Rx: 3   *When You Hear the Word, Do the Word*

Be a quick study. Don't hear the Word, then consult some commentaries, then think about it for ten years, then forget about it for ten years, then finally get around to partially doing it.

> Do not merely listen to the word, and so deceive yourselves. Do what it says. Anyone who listens to the word but does not do what it says

is like someone who looks at his face in a mirror and, after looking at himself, goes away and immediately forgets what he looks like. But whoever looks intently into the perfect law that gives freedom, and continues in it—not forgetting what they have heard, but doing it—they will be blessed in what they do."[12]

A Russian proverb reminds us, "There is no reason to accuse the mirror if you have a crooked face."

Rx: 4   *Live in Such a Way That if God Didn't Exist, Your Life Wouldn't Make Sense*

Cardinal Suhard, Archbishop of Paris, once wrote, "To be a witness does not consist in engaging in propaganda or even in stirring people up, but in being a living mystery; it means to live in such a way that one's life would not make sense if God did not exist." If God suddenly left and didn't tell anyone, do you think we would just carry on as before? Francis Schaeffer said, "If prayer and the Holy Spirit disappeared from the church in America it would be a long time before they were missed." What about our ministries? What about our churches? Are we dependent on prayer and the Spirit? Do we make space in our lives for the supernatural?

Rx: 5   *Don't Conform to the World*

The value structure of this world is very powerful, almost dictatorial. And it is nearly always in variance with the value structure found in the Scriptures. What to do? For many, if lifestyle and Scripture disagree, we compromise until they don't disagree any more.

While visiting a wonderful Christian man in the Southeast, I received a pen from his business. During dinner, for some reason, I was reflecting on humility, meekness, patience, gentleness, compassion, and other qualities taught in Colossians 3. He laughed. "Not in my business." I said, "What?" "Not in my business," he repeated. "I'd get killed." I gave him his pen back and told him to cross out Colossians 3 and all those other equally impossible verses in the Bible. He smiled and accepted my point, and we remain good friends.

Rx: 6   *Regard Authenticity as a Minute-by-Minute Proposition*

Authenticity is asking God to run our lives and meaning it. But let's continue down this road a bit further. What about God running our days? How about our hours and minutes? This is much more intriguing. We all say that we want God to run our *lives*, but running our *minutes* is a different proposition, and nothing less than walking in the Spirit. It sounds a bit too intimate for some, and yet authenticity itself is a minute-by-minute proposition. God is good at this. Yes, He is infinitely large, eternal, and the Ancient of Days, but that doesn't mean He can't do minutes, too. Such intimacy introduces us to regular promptings of the Spirit.

Rx: 7   *Avoid Interpersonal Comparisons*

Nothing is more inauthentic than continuously playing the comparison game: looks, hair, income, cars, clothes, grades, athletics, vacations, gardens. We do it all the time, and it often ends in one of two unfortunate ways. Either we come out badly and stew in our juices of self-pity, discontent with our inferior life; or we compare quite superiorly, thank you very much, and pat ourselves on the back for our good fortune, and for that matter, our own prowess in being a winner. Again.

Of course, usually we are just having fun. But at best, this is lateral motion and does nothing to move us in the direction of true authentic faith. Contentment says we sincerely thank God for each gift received regardless of others. If we notice someone has more, we thank God for their prosperity and wish them abundant ministry sharing those blessings. If someone has less, we develop a preferential and tender concern for them, quietly pledging in our hearts to lift them at every opportunity.

Rx: 8   *Live Ready, Continuously*

If death came today and knocked on our doors, most of us would be inclined to respond, "Give me a month to get ready." Get ready for what? To straighten out priorities? To begin living consistent with our beliefs? If *that* is what we need a month to prepare for, then why wait for death? Why not get ready now? Why not *live* ready? One of the great gifts of authenticity is that it leaves us continuously ready for whatever comes next.

THE BEST PART TO PLAY

C. S. Lewis, the brilliant professor of Medieval and Renaissance Literature at Cambridge, understood Shakespeare well. In one of Lewis' books, he described this scene:

> In *King Lear*, there is a man who is such a minor character that Shakespeare has not given him even a name: he is merely "First Servant." All the characters around him—Regan, Cornwall, and Edmund—have fine long-term plans. They think they know how the story is going to end, and they are quite wrong. The servant has no such delusions. He has no notion how the play is going to go. But he understands the present scene.

The First Servant, a bit character in the play, is in attendance and suddenly sees "an abomination taking place." An elderly man, Gloucester, is falsely accused and about to be blinded. The servant, who will not stand for the injustice, draws his sword to prevent it. Quickly, he is stabbed in the back and killed.

> That is his whole part: eight lines all told. But if it were real life and not a play, that is the part it would be best to have acted.[13]

Authenticity maintains that to do the right thing is always the right thing to do. Even if we are dead seconds later. It is a rigorous test of our contentment to accept a shortened life if righteousness requires it.

CHAPTER 12

ON FINAL APPROACH

Contentment on the Road Home

> Is it possible for people to miss their lives in the same way one misses a plane?
>
> — WALKER PERCY

The entire world is on a journey. Seven billion of us, continuously on the road.

It is impossible to delay the trip. We are being pulled forward by the most unbreakable law in the universe, the unrelenting tractor-beam of entropy. It always propels us straight ahead. We can't stop time, and we certainly can't back it up. Time's arrow always points to the future, and there is absolutely nothing we can do about it.

Some might protest, "When I'm sleeping I'm not going anywhere." As reasonable as this sounds, it is wrong. We remain on the road, along with our beds, even in stage-four sleep. In fact, the entire groaning, created universe is pulled on the same relentless journey.

Some religions teach that life is a circle, that in the end we keep dropping again into the hopper to be spit back out for another lap around the track. Other people think life simply ends, that we dissolve into a pointless and painless oblivion where worms eat our bodies and we wish them *bon appétit*.

The Christian story is different. We understand that this journey is linear, not cyclical. It has a beginning, a middle, and an end. It is a journey we take with God. We know He appears all along the timeline, intervening in history, creating, redeeming, sustaining. And He is purposed to get us safely home. He will not be denied.

Our journey is pulsing with meaning and throbbing with intentionality. This is not the nihilist vision of some existentialists, where nothingness had a seizure, spawned an absurd universe in a massive cosmic accident, filled us all with pain, and then will flicker out again, ending the farce.

Those who believe in a meaningless history have an insurmountable obstacle blocking their way: Jesus of Nazareth. In the fullness of time, He inserted Himself in the middle of the Middle East and in the middle of the massive Roman Empire, the "empire without end."

Nikolai Nikolaievich, Dr. Zhivago's uncle in Pasternak's novel, described it like this:

Rome was a flea market of borrowed gods and conquered peoples, a bargain basement on two floors, earth and heaven, a mass of filth convoluted in a triple knot as in an intestinal obstruction . . . heavy wheels without spokes, eyes sunk in fat, sodomy, double chins, illiterate emperors, fish fed on the flesh of learned slaves. There were more people in the world than there have ever been since, all crammed into the passages of the Coliseum, and all wretched.

And then, into this tasteless heap of gold and marble, He came, light and clothed in an aura, emphatically human, deliberately provincial, Galilean, and at that moment gods and nations ceased to be and man came into being—man the carpenter, man the plowman, man the shepherd with his flock of sheep at sunset, man who does not sound in the least proud, man thankfully celebrated in all the cradle songs of mothers and in all the picture galleries the world over.

The Messiah had landed. He grabbed history by the scruff of the neck, turned it upside down, and shook until the key fell out. He disrupted the religious and political orders, upended secure idols, and spread the good news throughout the entire world in a manner never before seen—using only the weapons of truth and love.

TWO DOWN, ONE TO GO

Despite the glorious "Act One: Creation," the Old Testament nonetheless stumbled to its concluding words, "Lest I come and smite the earth with a curse."[1] Then came "Act Two: Redemption." The Messiah turned everything around so radically that the New Testament ends quite differently. Now we find the words, "The grace of our Lord Jesus Christ be with you all."[2]

It was such a miraculous reversal, infinitely implausible, that we rightfully feel privileged to be on this side of the event. Still, we are not yet home. For that, we await the third and final act, the culmination of all things.

In the meantime, our journey continues. Here we are on the road—a very crowded road—all trying to figure it out. We talk among ourselves and learn that most are hot and tired. It hasn't rained in weeks and the farmers are desperate. For others, the bills keep coming but the money doesn't keep up. Quite a few are worried about their parents, or their children, or their grandkids. Many are not sure how they are going to afford college; others, retirement. There are so many demands on our time, our energy, and our wallets.

It is obvious many of these wayfarers don't want to be bothered with big questions. They are too busy and distracted. They just get up in the morning, get dressed, and do what is in front of them, trying to ignore their "baffled sense of drift." Even Bill Gates dodged it when asked about faith. "I don't have any evidence on that," he said. "Just in terms of allocation of time resources, religion is not very efficient. There's a lot more I could be doing on a Sunday morning."[3] Then he went back to his computers.

Others tell similar stories. Contentment means nothing to them and neither does God. They just want money, and lots of it. A thick wad in their wallet, an even thicker stash in their bank, and more than the next guy. Warren Buffett, for all his folksy manner, has been an intense moneyman. He was worth fifty billion at one time. Yet, for all that, he is a wounded billionaire. In 1977, he let his wife, Susan, walk away and it has grieved him ever since. She moved to California to get an apartment of her own and pursue singing. Mostly, though, it was caused by Buffett's busyness, being gone all the time, and his frequent east-coast "socializing" with Katharine Graham, publisher of *The Washington Post*.

Buffett later said Susan's leaving was the greatest failure of his life and 95 percent his fault. They remained good friends, and, at one point, she was among the top two hundred wealthiest people in the world with her stake in Buffett's company. He could hardly speak about her death without weeping. Even eight years after cancer took her life in 2004, he had to excuse himself from an interview to cry for a while. His views on success are authentic. It doesn't make any difference, he said, if you have a thousand dollars in the bank or a billion. If the people you want to love you actually do, you are a success.

Gates and Buffett, for all their lofty accomplishments, are on the same road we are, just two among the throng. Just like our neighbor down the street, and the eight-year-old, and the eighty-year-old, and the factory worker. The poor and the rich walk together. With regard to the journey, there is not a speck of difference. The tractor-beam keeps pulling us forward to the culmination.

Since we are fellow travelers, let me pose a question. If we could trade places with any of these other people, would we? How about those two guys over there, Bill Gates or Warren Buffett? Would any of us wish to change places with them? Tens of billions in the bank, outrageous success and respect, anything they want when they want it, giving millions to foundations — both agnostic, at best.

My own answer took less time than a Google search. "Thanks all the same. I'm content where I am." As a person of faith, I have not the slightest interest in going backward. Not even if you paid me a trillion dollars an hour.

SEEING THE UNSEEN

My quick response comes from an experience I had decades ago. In February 1969, I was at L'Abri in Huémoz, Switzerland, when God suddenly turned the lights on. Within a single day, He erased years of anguish by opening the windows of heaven. I saw, I understood, and all my questions were answered. It was as quick and easy as that.

Throughout this book, we have spoken about the unseen world and how the essence of reality is nonmaterial. God communicates within both the seen and unseen realms, and when He chooses to do so, it is effective. In my case, He adjusted the dial in my spirit. Previously I could hear nothing but static, and it was extremely frustrating. Suddenly, I clearly understood the signals coming from the other side. When before the unseen realm was hidden and silent, now it was brilliantly apparent and full of communication. It continued during my studies in Basel and throughout my hitchhiking/bus/train travels around Europe and the Middle East. It continued even when I was in Athens, a week late returning to school, and out of money. I was talking to God continuously and scooping large swathes of Scripture into my mouth. It was the most exhilarating time of my life.

Do you think I would trade that for a wheelbarrow full of green paper? The temptations from within our drab tunnel are listless compared to the glories of the heavenly domain. If we see both worlds side by side in true comparison, biblical contentment becomes a much easier choice.

Why would I wish to open a big bank account instead of opening the windows of heaven? Why would I wish to compare myself to others instead of comparing myself to Christlikeness? Why would I feel inferior about our simple life and older cars instead of agreeing with Tozer that I "have nothing to be ashamed of except sin"? Why would I complain about suffering instead of thanking the Father for making me a better and stronger person? Why would I murmur against the One who not only paid my gruesome debt but then set a place for me at His table? Why would I be discontent with my circumstances when "His divine power has given us everything we need for a godly life"?[4]

KINDNESS BEYOND MEASURE

It is hard to fully explain our continual lusting after earth rather than yearning for the beauty and perfection of heaven. It certainly doesn't help that we have such an insufficient and ill-formed vision of the glory outside our tunnel walls. I suppose that is why God comes inside to meet us. Our journey along the road is actually much more about the unseen reality than the visible world. From just beyond the shadows, God is continuously making His case.

No one has ever been courted like this. No one has ever been showered with gifts like this. He gave us a foundation on which to stand that is unmovable and unshakable. He gave us a vision that is staggeringly comprehensive. He gave us an inheritance sent on ahead that is not susceptible to market bubbles. He adopted us into His family. He grafted us in. He forgave us completely. He gave us the privilege of being joint heirs with Christ. He gave us unimpeded access to the throne room. He gave us Himself, the Christ, who came and walked among us so we could look God in the eye and get to know Him. He gave us the gift of His suffering, and He suffers with us still. He gave us His life and He gave us His death. He gave us His blood. He gave us the gift of the Cross and explained why it is bloody and why it is empty, along with the tomb. He paid the awful and complete penalty for sin. He gave us reconciliation. He gave us righteousness, by grace, even when we were far away. He gave us His friendship. He gave us fellowship. He gave us His patience. He measured faith to us. He gave us Truth. He gave us peace. He gave us the Word of God for our instruction. He gave us the Spirit of God for our encouragement. He gave us a Christian mind. He gave us a body crowned with glory and honor. He gave us another body, too, the body of believers. He gave us the Earth. He gave us the sun by day and the moon by night. He gave us the gift of nature so that we might see He is an artist who paints sunsets free of charge.

In other words, He gave us love.

Sounds like a pretty good deal, doesn't it?

If this is what we have been given, perhaps we can take a really bold risk and give Him a gift as well: our contentment. Who knows, it might turn out really well.

APPENDIX[1]

DYSFUNCTIONAL MATH

- More video is uploaded to YouTube in 60 days than all 3 major television networks created in 60 years.
- Google scientists counted over 1 trillion URLs (resources, documents, domain names) on the Web.
- The average American is exposed to 10 hours of media per day and watches 34 hours of television per week.
- Go to college and you can choose from over 500 baccalaureate degrees.
- Get a satellite dish and choose from over 1,000 movies a month.
- The average grocery store has 40,000 different products.
- There are 55,000 configurations of coffee at Starbucks.
- We each must learn to operate 20,000 pieces of equipment in our lifetime.
- In the next century, we will have a million times more technology than we do now.
- There are 400,000 books per year published in the U.S. and Great Britain.
- Artificial intelligence is increasing 10 million times faster than human intelligence.
- Knowledge workers check e-mail 50 times a day, use instant messaging 77 times a day, and visit 40 websites per day.
- The average desk worker starts something new every 3 minutes.
- Information overload costs businesses $650 billion/year and stress costs $300 billion/year.
- Information is increasing at a compound annual 60%.

- One third of us live with extreme stress, and 48% believe it has increased over the past 5 years (2008).
- There was more change in the last century than in all of recorded history prior to 1900.
- There will be a thousand times more change in this century than the last.
- Apple offers 650,000 apps in its Apps Store, and 30 billion apps have been downloaded.
- The new Fiat 500 subcompact has half a million combinations to choose from.
- Some new car owners' manuals are more than 800 pages.
- There are 90,000 governmental bodies in the U.S.
- U.S. businesses and households will spend over 7 billion hours complying with tax laws annually.
- In 1800 there was just 1 city with a million people; now there are 381.
- The percentages of households in the U.S. that are married-couple households: 1950–79%; 1960–74%; 1970–70%; 1980–61%; 1990–56%; 2000–52%; 2010–49.7%.
- At the turn of the twentieth century, the top 25 most populated cities in the world were in Europe and North America. Today, none is found in Europe and only two in North America: LA and NYC.
- People around the world spent a combined time of 200,000 years playing the smartphone game Angry Birds from its release in 2009 until the end of 2011.
- CERN, the new particle accelerator on the border of France and Switzerland, is the largest information generator in history, generating 1 billion particle interactions/second and creating 1 trillion bytes/second of information. This must be algorithmed down in 3 microseconds by a series of computers to a few hundred bytes, which are saved for future examination. All other bytes must be immediately jettisoned forever to make room for the next second's worth of data.

HEALTH CARE

- Health-care costs are now $2.6 trillion annually.
- Health care as a percentage of GDP: 1960–5.2%; 1970–7.2%; 1980–9.1%; 1990–12.3%; 2000–13.8%; 2012–17.8%.
- Doctors graduating from medical school owe an average of $155,000, while a quarter of new medical school grads owe over $200,000. It's not uncommon to hear of medical student debt over $400,000.
- At a recent staff meeting, we learned that the cost per minute for the OR was $88. If my math is correct, it amounts to $5,280 per hour.
- Ten thousand baby boomers will become eligible for Medicare every day for the next 19 years, causing the Medicare fiscal discrepancies to widen rapidly and unsustainably.
- Over the next 10 years, aging boomers will result in a 50% rise in the number of people 65–74 years old, a growth rate not seen in 50 years.
- Social Security, Medicare, and Medicaid make up 42% of the federal budget.
- Percentage of children in U.S. population, at 24%, is the lowest ever (in 1900–40%; 1980–28%; 1990–26%) — just when we need them the most to fund Medicare and Social Security.
- WebMD, with 22 million visitors per month, has a privacy statement link at the bottom of their home page, a 30-page explanation of how they will use your personal data.
- There are 35,000 publications a year in neuroscience, and no single researcher knows even 1% of that.
- The *Physicians' Desk Reference* has 3,300 pages; when first created in 1948, it had 300 pages.
- If I read 2 health-care-related articles every day for a year, next year at this time I would be a thousand years behind in my reading.

- The 1965 Medicare/Medicaid bill was 137 pages; 30 years later, there were over 130,000 pages of rules to comply with.
- The 1993 Clinton Healthcare Reform Act had 1,432 pages, called by one Democratic Senator "overwhelmingly complex, almost frighteningly complex."
- The current health-care reform act (Patient Protection & Affordable Care Act) is twice as large, at 2,800 pages and 400,000 words, making it the most complex and expensive legislative issue in U.S. history—and, if the multiplier holds, will result in millions of pages of regulations.
- In 1995, no state had an obesity rate above 20%; now every state does. The state with the lowest adult-obesity rate today would have had the highest rate in 1995.

ECONOMICS

- Total U.S. national debt: $16.5 trillion.
- GDP: $15.6 trillion.
- Gross debt to GDP: 106%.
- The federal debt is increasing $4 billion every day.
- Forty cents of every dollar the government spends is borrowed.
- U.S. total debt: $57 trillion (household, business, state government, local government, financial institutions, federal government).
- Total U.S. unfunded liability: $121 trillion (Social security–$16 trillion; prescription drug for Medicare–$21 trillion; Medicare–$83 trillion).
- Total student-loan debt: $1 trillion.
- American universities have raised their fees 5 times as fast as inflation over the past 30 years.
- The price of oil per barrel went from $25 up to $147 down to $33 and up to $112 in the past 10 years.

- Oil prices averaged $95 a barrel in 2011, gasoline $3.52 a gallon. A decade earlier, oil averaged $25 a barrel, while gasoline averaged $1.44 a gallon.
- Gas, which was between $1.00 and $1.20 during the entire decade of the 1990s, went to $4.01, then $1.87, then $4.00 in a span of 3 years.
- Since 1965, the GDP has increased 2.7 times, but entitlement expenses have increased 11.1 times.
- China, our largest creditor, holds $1.16 trillion of U.S. Treasury securities officially and likely as much as $2 trillion. Japan is second with $912 billion.
- In 2030, when the last of the baby boomers retire, there will be 77 million people on Medicare, up from 47 million today.
- In 2030, there will be 2.3 workers per retiree, compared to 3.4 today and about 4 when the program was created.
- U.S. household debt as a percentage of annual disposable personal income was 127% at the end of 2007, versus 77% in 1990.
- In 1981, U.S. private debt was 123% of GDP; by the third quarter of 2008, it was 290%.
- The cost of raising a child to age 18 is now $235,000, 40% greater than a decade ago.
- Since the housing bubble burst in 2006 and until mid-2012, home prices have fallen 32.6% nationwide.
- Value of all mortgaged property nationwide is $12.2 trillion; outstanding debt on those properties is $8.6 trillion. Thus, 70.5% of the value of all mortgaged homes is in debt.

NOTES

Chapter 1: The Freedom of Contentment

1. Matthew 19:14.
2. John Stumbo, *An Honest Look at a Mysterious Journey* (Fox Island, WA: Nesting Tree Books, 2011), 127.
3. 1 Corinthians 13:12, KJV.
4. John 8:23.
5. See Hebrews 10:35–11:40.
6. Hebrews 11:1, KJV.
7. See Romans 1:19-20.
8. Exodus 33:20.
9. See 2 Corinthians 4:17.
10. See 1 Corinthians 13:12, KJV.
11. Psalm 91:1.

Chapter 2: Jesus and Contentment

1. John 6:5-6.
2. See John 21:15-17.
3. See Matthew 16:13-20.
4. Luke 24:17.
5. Luke 24:32.
6. Mark 2:1: "A few days later, when Jesus again entered Capernaum, the people heard that he had come home." Such passages, however, are not conclusive that this is anything more than coming back to Capernaum.

7. Matthew 8:20; Luke 9:58.

8. See Luke 8:1-3.

9. See Matthew 17:24-27.

10. See John 12:4-6; 13:29.

11. John 1:46.

12. See Luke 4:29.

13. John 1:49.

14. John 7:15.

15. John 4:31-34.

16. Matthew 4:2-4.

17. Saul, 1 Samuel 9:2; David, 1 Samuel 16:12; Absalom, 2 Samuel 14:25-26 and 18:9-15; Zacchaeus, Luke 19:3-4.

18. See Isaiah 53:2.

19. Deuteronomy 17:16-17.

20. C. S. Lewis, *God in the Dock: Essays on Theology and Ethics* (Grand Rapids, MI: Eerdmans, 1972), 182.

21. Matthew 5:3-12.

22. Matthew 6:25-34, emphasis added.

23. See Exodus 20:17.

24. Luke 12:13-21, esv.

25. Matthew 6:19-20.

26. John 15:5.

27. John 14:27.

28. John 16:33.

29. Luke 6:46.

Chapter 3: Contentment in History

1. Psalm 131:1-2.

2. Psalm 131:2, gw.

3. Psalm 73:2-3,23-25.

4. Proverbs 19:23.

5. Proverbs 30:8-9.

6. Habakkuk 3:17-19.

7. Brother Yun and Paul Hattaway, *The Heavenly Man: The Remarkable True Story of Chinese Christian Brother Yun* (Carlisle UK: Piquant, 2003), 286–287.

Chapter 4: The Modern De-Emphasis of Contentment

1. Ozymandias is the Greek name for Ramesses II (1303–1213 BC), a mighty Pharaoh of Egypt during the thirteenth century BC. The quote used is in reference to Percy Bysshe Shelley's poem "Ozymandias," written in 1818.
2. Barbara W. Tuchman, *A Distant Mirror: The Calamitous 14th Century* (New York: Ballantine Books, 1979), xiii–xx, 3–48.
3. Progress works by differentiation, proliferation, combination, invention, and discovery. As a result, it always results in more and more of everything faster and faster. This process is extraordinarily important because it drives our future and its accompanying dysfunctions. This process has been described in three of my earlier books: *Margin* (Colorado Springs, CO: NavPress, 2004), 21–33; *The Overload Syndrome* (Colorado Springs, CO: NavPress, 2004), 39–48; *In Search of Balance* (Colorado Springs, CO: NavPress, 2010), 32–43.
4. Aaron Souppouris, "IBM's Sequoia earns 'world's fastest supercomputer' title," TheVerge.com, June 18, 2012, http://articles.washingtonpost.com/2012-06-18/business/35461247_1_fastest-supercomputer-petaflops-supercomputer-list.
5. Rana Foroohar, "The Great Wall Street Sucking Sound," *TIME*, April 4, 2011.
6. J. Hudson Taylor, *Hudson Taylor* (Minneapolis: Bethany House, 1987), 21, 25–27.

Chapter 5: The Secret of Contentment

1. Keith Getty and Stuart Townend, "In Christ Alone," Kingsway Thankyou Music, 2001.
2. Acts 22:3.
3. See Acts 7:55-58.

4. Acts 9:1-2.

5. Acts 20:24.

6. See Acts 14, 16, 21; 1 Corinthians 4; 2 Corinthians 4, 6, 11.

7. 2 Corinthians 4:17.

8. Philippians 4:11-12.

9. Jeremiah Burroughs, *The Rare Jewel of Christian Contentment* (Edinburgh, Scotland: The Banner of Truth Trust, 1648, 1987), 17–18.

10. John 15:5.

11. Colossians 3:2.

12. Psalm 62:10.

13. Matthew 6:21.

14. Douglas Taylor, "Contentment," Works Worth Declaring, January 18, 2012, http://worksworthdeclaring.blogspot.com/2012/01/contentment.html.

15. Peter Ainslie, *God and Me* (New York: Revell, 1908), 31.

16. Matthew Henry, "Pray for the Graces of Contentment and Patience," http://www.matthewhenry.org/article/pray-for-the-graces-of-contentment-and-patience.

17. Matthew Henry, *Commentary on the Whole Bible*, 2 Kings 6, http://www.biblestudytools.com/commentaries/matthew-henry-complete/2-kings/6.html?p=5.%20Commentary%20on%202%20Kings%206:24-33.

18. Psalm 25:14, NASB.

19. Isaiah 45:15.

20. Matthew 13:11; see also verses 34-35.

21. Matthew 11:25.

22. See John 15:1-8.

23. Philippians 3:13-14.

24. Sylvia Gunter, *You Are Blessed in the Names of God* (Birmingham, AL: The Father's Business, 2008), 72.

25. See Luke 9:23.

Chapter 6: Godliness with Contentment

1. Isaiah 61:3: "They will be called *oaks of righteousness*, a planting of the LORD for the display of his splendor," emphasis added.
2. 1 Samuel 2:30.
3. John 1:16, ESV.
4. 1 Timothy 6:7-8.
5. Matthew 6:25.
6. Matthew 6:31-32.
7. 1 Timothy 6:9-10, emphasis added.
8. 1 Timothy 6:11-12.
9. Ephesians 3:8.
10. 2 Corinthians 8:9.
11. James 2:5.
12. Matthew 6:20-21, KJV.
13. 1 Timothy 6:17-19.
14. 1 Peter 5:5; James 4:10; Matthew 23:12; Ephesians 4:2; Philippians 2:3.
15. Philippians 2:9; see also verses 5-11.
16. See 1 Peter 1:3-5,7,18-19.

Chapter 7: Be Content . . . Because God

1. Editor, "Life of the Author," in Thomas Vincent, *The True Christian's Love to the Unseen Christ* (New York: James Eastburn, 1812), 5, http://books.google.com/books?id=e18XAAAAYAAJ& printsec=frontcover&source=gbs_ge_summary_r&cad=0#v= onepage&q=weaken%20hands&f=false.
2. Thomas Vincent, *God's Terrible Voice in the City* (Bridgeport: Lockwood & Backus, 1811), 12, 13, 16–17, 19, http://books .google.com/books?id=_WoPAAAAYAAJ&printsec=frontcover& source=gbs_ge_summary_r&cad=0#v=onepage&q&f=false.
3. Vincent, *God's Terrible Voice in the City*, 30.
4. Vincent, *God's Terrible Voice in the City*, 49–50.
5. Vincent, *The True Christian's Love to the Unseen Christ*, 64–65.
6. See Revelation 6:1-8.

7. See Romans 8:38-39.

8. A literal translation of this verse is rendered, "Without covetousness the behaviour, being content with the things present, for He hath said, 'No, I will not leave, no, nor forsake thee'" (Young's Literal Translation).

9. Romans 7:7-8.

10. The seven deadly sins, also known as the seven cardinal sins or seven capital sins, are greed, pride, sloth, lust, wrath, gluttony, and envy.

11. Proverbs 14:30.

12. See 1 Corinthians 13:4.

13. James 3:16-18.

14. Marvin Olasky, "Battling Class Envy: A Long Struggle for Me, and for America," *WORLD*, October 22, 2011, 76.

15. George Sanchez, "How to Succeed God's Way," *Discipleship Journal* 17, October 1983.

Chapter 8: Contentment and Simplicity

1. Jon Myhre, "Remember the Power," *Get Satisfied: How Twenty People Like You Found the Satisfaction of Enough*, ed. Carol Holst (Westport, CT: Easton Studio Press, 2007), 73–78.

2. Hebrews 12:1.

3. Isaiah 55:2.

4. C. S. Lewis, *Surprised by Joy: The Shape of My Early Life* (New York: Harcourt Brace, 1955), 201.

5. Elinore Pruitt Stewart, *Letters of a Woman Homesteader* (Mineola, NY: Dover, 1913 and 2006), 89.

6. Greg Smith, "Shoppers Are Making More Purchasing Decisions In-Store Than Ever Before," May 9, 2012, The Global Association for Marketing at Retail, http://www.popai.com/engage/?p=52.

7. Herb Weisbaum, "Impulse purchases continue to bust budgets," MSNBC.com, June 7, 2012, http://lifeinc.today.msnbc.msn .com/_news/2012/06/07/12069307-impulse-purchases-continue -to-bust-budgets.

8. Ken Murray, "How Doctors Die: It's Not Like the Rest of Us, but It Should Be," Zócalo Public Square, http://zocalopublicsquare .org/thepublicsquare/2011/11/30/how-doctors-die/read/nexus/.

9. Richard A. Swenson, *In Search of Balance: Keys to a Stable Life* (Colorado Springs, CO: NavPress, 2010), 112–116, 126–127.

10. See Hebrews 12:1-3.

11. 2 Corinthians 11:3, KJV.

12. Proverbs 20:19.

13. 1 Thessalonians 4:11.

14. Isaiah 30:15.

15. Philippians 2:5-8, NASB.

16. The Editors of Paraclete Press, *The Paraclete Book of Hospitality* (Brewster, MA: Paraclete Press, 2012), 15–19.

17. Colossians 3:12.

Chapter 9: Contentment and Money

1. Anuj Chopra, "In Man vs. Rat, the Humans Get a New Edge," *U.S. News & World Report*, January 8, 2008, 25.

2. "Despite Woes, Conflicts, World a Happier Place Than in 2007 as 22% (+2 points) of Global Citizens Say They're 'Very Happy'," Ipsos-NA.com, February 9, 2012, http://www.ipsos-na.com/news -polls/pressrelease.aspx?id=5515. Very happy is "a key measure that identifies comparative depth and intensity of happiness among country citizens and the world. Whereas the general assess- ment of happiness tends to remain fairly static over time, the measure of those who are 'very happy' has the greatest amount of fluctuation."

3. "Nigeria Tops Happiness Survey," BBC News, October 2, 2003, http://news.bbc.co.uk/2/hi/africa/3157570.stm.

4. "2011 Quality of Life Index," *International Living*, http://www1.internationalliving.com/qofl2011/.

5. "List of Countries by GDP (PPP) per Capita," U.S. $48,387; Nigeria $2,578, http://en.wikipedia.org/wiki/List_of_countries _by_GDP_(PPP)_per_capita.

6. "Money Can Buy *Some* Happiness," *The Week*, September 24, 2010, 24. This is a discussion of a Gallup survey of 450,000 people analyzed by two Princeton economists.

7. Peter Stanford, "So What Does Kirsty Young Mean by 'Being Content'?" January 24, 2012, *The Telegraph*, http://www .telegraph.co.uk/family/9035926/So-what-does-Kirsty-Young -mean-by-being-content.html.

8. Jonathan Edwards, "Full Contentment in Christ," Free Grace Broadcaster: Contentment 213, 14–17, http://www.chapellibrary .org/files/archive/pdf-english/contfg.pdf.

9. Acts 20:35.

10. Matthew 6:24.

11. Deuteronomy 8:17-18.

12. 1 John 3:17, ESV.

13. Lam Thuy Vo, "How Much Does the Government Spend to Send a Kid to Public School?" June 12, 2012, NPR, http://www.npr .org/blogs/money/2012/06/21/155515613/how-much-does-the -government-spend-to-send-a-kid-to-school.

14. Schumpeter, "How to Make College Cheaper," *The Economist*, July 7, 2011, http://www.economist.com/node/18926009.

15. Philip Aldrick, "IMF Warns US, Eurozone Deficits a Threat to Stability," *The Telegraph*, June 18, 2011, http://www.telegraph .co.uk/finance/economics/8583008/IMF-warns-US-eurozone -deficits-a-threat-to-stability.html.

16. Lawrence Summers, "How to Avoid Our Own Lost Decade," *Financial Times*, June 12, 2011, http://www.ft.com/cms/ s/2/b3c143b6-952d-11e0-a648-00144feab49a.html #axzz26AHGX0rZ.

17. "States with the Most Homes Underwater," *24/7 Wall St.*, July 19, 2012, http://247wallst.com/2012/07/19/states-with-the-most -homes-underwater/.

18. "In Plato's Cave," *The Economist*, January 27, 2009, 10, quoting Goldman's chief financial officer, David Viniar.

19. 1 Timothy 6:10.

20. Proverbs 3:5.

21. Proverbs 11:28.

22. 1 John 2:15-17.

23. Al Weir, MD, "One Kobo," CMDA Weekly Devotion, May 15, 2012.

Chapter 10: Contentment and Suffering

1. Information taken from CMDA *Christian Doctor's Digest*, November 2005, Dr. Elaine Eng interviewed by Dr. David Stevens; from her book *A Christian Approach to Overcoming Disability: A Doctor's Story* (Binghamton, NY: The Haworth Pastoral Press, 2004); and from personal conversations.

2. Romans 5:3-5.

3. See Psalm 103:13.

4. John R. W. Stott, "Suffering God," *Christianity Today*, March 5, 2007, http://www.christianitytoday.com/ct/2007/march/27.71.html.

5. 1 Peter 5:8-9.

6. See 1 Corinthians 10:13.

7. See Mark 8:31.

8. Hebrews 2:10: "In bringing many sons to glory, it was fitting that God, for whom and through whom everything exists, should make the author of their salvation perfect through suffering."

9. Hebrews 2:18: "Because he himself suffered when he was tempted, he is able to help those who are being tempted."

10. Romans 8:17.

11. Philippians 3:10.

12. 1 Peter 4:1.

13. 1 Peter 4:12-13.

14. 2 Corinthians 12:10, ESV.

15. Acts 20:24.

16. Galatians 6:2.

17. James 1:2-4, NASB.

18. Romans 5:3-5.

19. 1 Peter 4:13; see also verses 12-16.

20. Aleksandr I. Solzhenitsyn, "A World Split Apart," Commencement Address delivered at Harvard University, June 8, 1978.

21. Francis Frangipane, *The Stronghold of God* (Lake Mary, FL: Charisma House, 1998), 45.

22. Norman Grubb, *C. T. Studd: Cricketer and Pioneer* (Fort Washington, PA: CLC Publications, 1993), 201–203, in "Passing on the Torch," Charity Ministries, http://www.charityministries.org/missions/newsletter/2006/August/newsletter-August2006-torch.a5w.

Chapter 11: Contentment and Authenticity

1. Tim Ellsworth, "Ahmad Miller gets NFL spot from Rich Williams' integrity," Baptist Press, May 14, 2002, http://www.bpnews.net/bpnews.asp?id=13366.

2. Chuck Colson, "The Right Thing to Do: The Gil Meche Story," February 8, 2011, http://www.breakpoint.org/bpcommentaries/entry/13/16357; Tyler Kepner, "Pitcher Spurns $12 Million to Keep Self-Respect," *New York Times*, January 26, 2011; "Gil Meche: Saying No to $12.4 Million," *The Week*, February 11, 2011, 21.

3. Psalm 17:3.

4. Mark Thoma, "Money for Nothing: Pretending to Take the Bait," *Economist's View*, April 1, 2006, http://economistsview.typepad.com/economistsview/2006/04/money_for_nothi.html.

5. Jeffrey Heller, "Clerics clash in Church of the Nativity," Reuters, December 28, 2011, http://www.reuters.com/article/2011/12/28/us-palestinians-church-idUSTRE7BR0EN20111228; "Clergymen fight with brooms at Church of the Nativity in Bethlehem," *The Telegraph*, December 28, 2011, http://www.telegraph.co.uk/news/religion/8980618/Clergymen-fight-with-brooms-at-Church-of-the-Nativity-in-Bethlehem.html.

6. "Village atheist—and pastor," *WORLD*, June 21, 2003, 10.

7. Psalm 119:1.

8. Psalm 139:2-4.

9. Psalm 51:10.

10. See 1 Corinthians 13:1-3.

11. See Matthew 22:36-40.

12. James 1:22-25.

13. C. S. Lewis, *The Essential C. S. Lewis*, Lyle W. Dorsett, ed. (New York: Simon & Schuster, 1996/1988), 388. This scene regards King Lear, Act III, Scene vii, in C. S. Lewis' *The World's Last Night*.

Chapter 12: On Final Approach

1. Malachi 4:6, KJV.

2. Revelation 22:21, KJV.

3. John Lofton, "Warren Buffett 'Agnostic,' Bill Gates Rejects Sermon on the Mount, Not 'Huge Believer' in 'Specific Elements' of Christianity," The American View, http://archive.theamericanview .com/index.php?id=649.

4. 2 Peter 1:3.

Appendix: Dysfunctional Math

1. A continuously updated Dysfunctional Math listing with sources can be found at RichardSwenson.com.

ABOUT THE AUTHOR

RICHARD A. SWENSON, MD, is a physician-futurist, best-selling author, and award-winning educator. He received his BS in physics (Phi Beta Kappa) from Denison University (1970) and his MD from the University of Illinois School of Medicine (1974). Following five years of private practice, in 1982 Dr. Swenson accepted a teaching position as associate clinical professor with the University of Wisconsin medical school system Department of Family Medicine, where he taught for fifteen years. He currently is a full-time futurist, physician-researcher, author, and educator. As a physician, his focus is "cultural medicine," researching the intersection of health and culture. As a futurist, his emphasis is fourfold: the future of the world system, Western culture, faith, and health care.

Dr. Swenson has traveled extensively (to fifty-five countries, living abroad for a total of three years), including a year of study in Europe and medical work in developing countries. He is the author of seven books, including the best-selling *Margin: Restoring Emotional, Physical, Financial, and Time Reserves to Overloaded Lives* and *The Overload Syndrome: Learning to Live Within Your Limits*, both award winning.

He has written and presented widely, both nationally and internationally, on the themes of margin, stress, overload, life balance, complexity, societal change, health care, and future trends. A representative listing of presentations includes a wide variety of career, professional, educational, governmental, and management groups; most major church denominations and organizations; and members of the United Nations, Congress, NASA, and the Pentagon. He was an invited guest participant for the 44th Annual National Security Seminar.

Dr. Swenson has given presentations to national medical conferences such as the American Academy of Family Physicians, the American Association of Occupational Medicine, the American Society of Prospective Medicine, the general medical staff of the Mayo Clinic, as well as hundreds of other national, regional, state, and local medical settings. He also has researched extensively and written on the future of health care, helping to initiate a national multidisciplinary group examining the health-care crisis and exploring new paradigms. In 2002, he was awarded the National Leadership Award from the Central States Occupational Medical Association for his original work on margin and overload. In 2003, he was awarded Educator of the Year Award by Christian Medical and Dental Associations.

Dr. Swenson and his wife, Linda, live in Menomonie, Wisconsin. They have two sons, Matthew (and Suzie) and Adam (and Maureen), and a granddaughter, Katja.

INDEX